THE BLUEPRINT

Developing Your DNA for Success

JULIAN YOUNG

Order this book online at www.trafford.com
or email orders@trafford.com

Most Trafford titles are also available at major online book retailers.

Trafford rev. 06/12/2012

 www.trafford.com

North America & international
toll-free: 1 888 232 4444 (USA & Canada)
phone: 250 383 6864 ♦ fax: 812 355 4082

CONTENTS

DEDICATION

Firstly, I dedicate this book to God, my Father, who has taught me the value of patience, being still, enduring seasons, and maintaining vision. Your love is extravagant and it's the spiritual steam that drives me everyday. Thank you for comfort in the times I felt like giving up, for listening even in my moments of complaining and for giving me chance after chance to become the man I've always wanted to be through the abundant Grace of your Son. Thank you for teaching me the Kingdom and how to expect from myself the same things you expect out of me.

I would also like to dedicate this book to my mentor, spiritual father, advisor, and friend, Bishop James Anderson, who during the process of creating this book went home to be with Lord. Your impact in my life has been truly immeasurable and unforgettable. It was through our connection that I learned the true meaning of sonship and began to fully embrace the path of Destiny. May your wisdom, through me, continue to echo throughout the generations to come. Thank you Bishop for your priceless investment into my life, humanity and to this world.

Lastly, I dedicate this book to my amazing wife and best friend, Brittany Ann Young. You are the most valuable person in my life and my first and most important ministry. Thank you for taking a chance on me, for believing in the God in me and the vision in my heart. I love you dearly, and words are unjustifiable when trying to articulate my gratitude for your love, patience and support. This is "our" project and I am forever grateful to have worked with you on this. It is the first of many and I look forward to building the Kingdom of God with you.

INTRODUCTION

Life by Design: The Blueprint

Merriam Webster's dictionary defines a *limitation* as: "being confined or having restriction; something that limits a quality or achievement." Our world today is filled with "I can't" and "I'll never" philosophies that govern most people's thinking, and our media outlets constantly reinforce what we can and can't do, which fosters what I call the "survivalist mentality." Rather than thriving people have set their bar of success to simply just surviving. Others have become so afraid to fail at life they aren't playing to win they are playing not to lose. Therefore, the concept of a life without limits has become a lost ideology.

With all of these contradictions around us is it possible to still defy the laws of fear, religion and humanistic thinking? Is it still possible to defy the laws of "gravity" and live life on your own terms? The answer is absolutely, yes! When God created the world and established the laws of creation He designed every single creature and its system to operate within some type of confine and boundary, except for the man. This is because God created, designed and shaped man in His image to be a direct reflection of Him in the earth.

This means that all of the ingenuity, creativity, wittiness, and intelligence of God was downloaded into man when God decided to create Him. In doing so God "blessed him" or gave him His divine life pattern for success. That "Blessing" was more than a favorable word spoken; it was the unlimited and unhindered complete influence of Heaven placed into Adam to manifest God's image (nature, laws, culture, and authority) in the earth. That image is His pattern. A pattern is defined as: a form or model purposed for imitation; something designed or used as a model for making things. The Blessing is God's ultimate life model for man, a systematic arrangement of laws, principles and power that when applied can defy any limitation in life.

Stop and think for a moment that this was truly God's original intention when He created you, the essential idea that inspired your existence! I have even better news: God has not stopped thinking about the limitless life He predestined and planned for you since the beginning! Look at Jeremiah 29:11:

> *["For I know the plans I have for you," declares the LORD, "plans to prosper you and not to harm you, plans to give you hope and a future."]*

The word "plan" in Hebrew terminology expresses intention and purpose, as in the original idea or thought that has inspired something. It is the same idea for "Word" in the Greek, known as "logos" which we find in John 1:1, *"In the beginning was the Word and the Word was God."*

Logos also means reason, plan or thought. What God is trying to communicate to us through Jeremiah 29:11 is that He is still focused on the original idea that transpired before we were ever born.

At the time God made this statement it was extremely powerful, because the children of Israel had just been taken into captivity by Babylon in which they would remain for seventy years. Even in their darkest time God continued speaking to them about the original vision He had for their lives. This is how God thinks toward you. I can tell you with the utmost confidence that God is never thinking anything bad about you! Why? Well, for two reasons: 1) Jesus' blood settled all wrath and has given you victory and peace with God. 2) He is still consumed by His enormous plan to prosper you, not to harm you. He made it clear that no matter the consequences we face in life He is still focused on accomplishing His original goal for our lives. God tells us things like this for three reasons: 1) He wants us to know how much He loves us and desires for us to excel beyond all limits. 2) He wants us to think like Him. 3) He wants us to see what He sees, so that we can come into agreement with Him about the incredible plan He has in store for us. When God said, "prosper," He meant to excel and thrive beyond all normalcy, confines and basic capacities of life. Whether spiritually, physically, emotionally, or financially, God's blueprint is a guaranteed model for success in every area of your life.

The key to tapping into this "blessed" life begins with recognizing that you are living in a world ruled by another system and another way of life. You must learn to leverage God's Blessing to break free from its boundaries. The world's system operates a lot like the Kingdom of God in that it functions by laws and principles also. It is a fallen system called "the cursed world system." In other words, it is a life completely unattached to God. It is ruled with its own philosophies, ideas, culture, and ideologies, which mostly reinforce fear, worry, doubt, and the limitations of man. All of these characteristics exist outside of God, and that's exactly what this system is intended to do, inspire the idea of life independent from its Creator. This fallen paradigm or "way of living" was introduced to Adam after he decided to relinquish himself of God's Kingdom (Genesis 3:10-12, 13-24) for what he thought was a better one (Genesis 3:4-6).

Since man didn't truly realize how much he was like God and how much of Himself God had invested into him, he aborted his lifestyle in hopes of something better. Sadly this has been the state of many believers today. The message of God's Kingdom and His Blessing have been wrongly communicated, so people do not truly understand the creative power that is within them. They fail to realize how much like God they truly are. The reality is we have the unlimited and sovereign power of Christ's internal kingship inside of us. That's why Philippians 2:6 reads:

[Who, being in the form (image) of God, thought it not robbery to be equal with God.]

Christ knew who He was in God, but He also had a clearly defined understanding of His relationship to God. The scriptures remind us that Christ sits at the "right hand of God." In ancient kingdoms, being seated at the right side of a king symbolized equal authority. It meant that even though the king was supreme, he considered you an equal dignitary. This is how God sees us: *in Christ*. We are seated at His right hand too (Ephesians 2:6).

If we have Christ, who is the image of God, then we ought not think it robbery to be counted equal to Jesus. This is what He wants. Jesus came not to be our father, but our brother (Mark 3:33). Why? He came to add brothers to His royal family to share in the royal dynasty (Romans 8:29-30). In doing this He could expand the rule and the influence of His Father's Kingdom. Why do you think we were raised and seated with Him in the Heavenly kingdoms? (Celestial, means the highest ranking Kingdom.) Why do you think we are called "co-creators or co-heirs" with Christ? It's all pointing to the original vision and purpose God had for His creation of man: to be His impression and extension of His glory in the earth.

If we are not careful, the spiritual gravity of our own insecurities will cause us to be afraid of seeing who God really created us to be. We are His sons. Don't be afraid of who you are in Jesus as God's royal family.

We aren't just an example, but an exact representation of Him: *"In His image!"* If we are going to live above every limitation and natural law of life, we have to destroy the erroneous idea and defeated mentalities that are floating around in Christendom. Christ's Kingdom is all inclusive of His power, honor, authority, and rule. He didn't leave anything out in His Blessing. He gave us His perfect life, His perfect peace and His unlimited paradigm to think, live and function in for the display of His glory.

The Righteous Solution

When we leave this authoritative part of dominion out of Christ's message, people are not able to see how the Kingdom can practically impact their lives now. They don't see a solution when they look at the Kingdom; they mostly see religion, because that is all that has been presented. So, rather than trust in what they cannot see value in, they unconsciously return to a system that is mentality governed by fear and toilsome labor (Genesis 3:17-19).

The Kingdom is a *now* message; it is a solution for your everyday life. Do you notice that when you listen to the news the majority of what you hear about is recession, financial crisis, job cuts, and almost every negative thing that's going on in society today? Why is it that when you turn on the news they are never telling you about how the financial crisis doesn't matter or that you can do anything if you put your mind to it? Why doesn't the newsperson, after reporting negative statistics about job losses, periodically pause and tell you that even if you lost your job you can get back up and failure isn't your final authority? This is because it is a system designed to keep you thinking lowly and defeated about yourself.

The truth is they can't tell you anything positive because they neither see nor believe there is a positive solution. In their minds it's, "Here are the statistics. This is how it is and there isn't anything you can do about it."

However, in the Kingdom of God there is always a solution and a plan to overcome. As long as you have the unlimited power of

Heaven's throne in you it is waiting to be unleashed and to explode in your life. You are never subject to negative circumstances that surround you. There is always a higher word that can supersede what has been previously spoken about you. If you are going to take the limits off of your life, you must start with believing deep in your heart that God has already given you everything you need to prosper and excel in every realm of life. Philippians 4:19 states:

> *[And this same God who takes care of me will supply all your needs from his glorious riches, which have been given to us in Christ Jesus.]*

I've heard this scripture all my life growing up, but it never really impacted me until I learned about the Kingdom I inherited through Christ Jesus. When I began to understand that we automatically receive the Kingdom when we receive Christ, my life began to radically change. You see, when we realize this truth we tap into the actualization of God's abundant life in us and we gain unlimited access to the riches and endless supply of Heaven.

God's Kingdom is the solution to everything that is out of alignment in your life. There isn't one problem in your life that cannot be fixed through the Blessing. The Blessing is synonymous with God's peace or *shalom*, meaning "nothing missing, nothing broken or left out." Jesus said "And you will know the truth (and apply it) and that truth (that you apply) will set you free." Those truths flow from the unhindered place of Christ's Kingship, which come through wisdom and understanding.

So through intense Kingdom training God is trying to reawaken us to the unlimited and unhindered lifestyle of Adam; experiencing God's best for you every single day of your life. That "best life" includes all of the benefits of your royal inheritance and the ability to function beyond any capacity in both your physical and spiritual realities, now! If you desire that life and can sense there is more to what you've been experiencing in Christianity, change is about to come for you. I wrote this book for people who are hungry to experience a greater dimension of God's love, provision, destiny, and abundance. Don't believe the limitations you are faced with or the negative reinforcements that surround you. You aren't waiting for any particular time to start prospering beyond your imagination; you are waiting for the right information to be applied in your life. You are waiting to break free from a "fallen paradigm" and to be reawakened to the realization of Heaven's atmosphere in your heart. God's Kingdom can change your life now, but only with careful and skillful consistency in the application of His Word.

The Quality of Life Design

According to Hebrews 11:10, God is not only our creator, He is the "chief architect" and the "master builder" of our lives. These expressions not only imply the creative mastery and ingenuity involved when setting out to build a house or structure, but they also imply the strategic planning process that takes place before a single layer of the foundation has been applied. Can you imagine God, the chief architect of creation, dwelling in the shadows of eternity designing, orchestrating, and constructing your life?

Amazingly, though you may not realize it, when God thought of you He thought of Himself. He imagined everything about you. How you would look, talk, your smile, and all of your unique qualities that make up the person you are. He carefully took His time uniquely crafting and skillfully mapping out His ultimate plan for your life. That plan was to give you a life that would reflect all of His goodness. That's right, your life is intended to express the very best of God and His supreme nature. Do you think that His plan has somehow changed? Does God expect anything different out of your life now, other than what He created it for? No! His expectation is still the same and His desire is for that same hope to be the core driving force of your life and success.

God created you to dominate and excel beyond the normal perimeters of life. He wants you to break outside the "box!" That's why it's important that we dig within ourselves to access God's infinite creativity hidden deep inside, so that we can live out *His* plan for our life rather than just our own. You see, as long as you aren't living out of God's original intended plan, you're always going to be hindered by your vision and limited to only what *you* can see. God's plan doesn't have any confines, and it will show you just how capable you really are of defying the odds of life.

Have you ever felt hindered in your faith and vision as though something was constantly holding you back? Have you continually struggled to break through in your life, business or journey to success? Life is filled with these obstacles set in place by negative forces intended to keep you from achieving your dreams. Understanding God's immense vision and purpose for you will help to propel you beyond all limitations. When God breathed into man He made an expensive investment: it was an extension of Himself. He gave you His life flow, His divine pattern and life source to empower you to live your most compelling life. That's true prosperity: the point at which we live our most compelling life. That pattern is like a blueprint, God's systematic way of living, which produces the atmosphere of Heaven in your life. What if you could live supernaturally out of Heaven's benefits while still remaining in the earth realm? Is that possible? Yes, and that is the destiny of every believer.

The more conscious you become of this inner "blueprint" you'll realize it's simply waiting there for you to tap into. The sooner you tap in, you can access the tangible power of God flowing through you so that you can experience life the way He always intended. That tangible power is God's Blessing, which is the system for duplicating God's lifestyle. The Kingdom exists for one reason: to help you get results in life *now!* By breaking into the Blessing you'll activate the

Kingdom's reality, releasing the blueprint of Heaven in your heart for you to live out of.

This was always God's plan. When He decided to "design" you in His image and likeness, He wanted you to have His way of life. By giving you His blueprint He made a contract to share with you all of His secrets, thoughts, and strategies for living. God's desire is for you to live out the perfection of His life pattern and reproduce His "image" in the earth.

You see, a personal relationship with God should go beyond the basic and normal parameters of church, prayer, and occasional encounters with our Creator. Rather a relationship with our King should consist of the most intimate knowledge of His thoughts, desires, and design for our everyday life. Why? Because you were created in His thoughts. Your relationship with Him only becomes fulfilling when you learn that He desires to have a constant exchange of thoughts and ideas with you. In this type of relationship the actual active and authentic presence of God in our lives takes form, making His pre-intended living arrangement for us inescapable. The most intimate parts of God are His thoughts. When God decided to create man in His image, this preceded the idea and formation of the Heavens and the earth. God thought of you before all of this.

Now, the word *image* can also be translated to mean *scheme*. This gives the impression of architecture and structure, sort of like a blueprint. Secondly, *image* implies His thoughts and creative imagination. That's why the word *imagination* derives from the word *image*. God's expectation for our lives flows from His creative inspiration where no boundaries exist. His creative thought and unlimited imagination are the source from which your very existence derives.

Just as a picture captured by the photogenic rays of light has to be developed in the dark, so God, in the secret place of His thoughts developed His *image* and plan for you. When God suggests to Jeremiah that He *knew* him before he was formed in his mother's womb, that word *knew* literally means *intimacy*, as in sexual intercourse.

God was trying to communicate to Jeremiah that even before he became a tiny seed germinating within the entrails of his mother's womb, He previously had intimate dealings with him. From His creative personality to unlimited potential and ruling authority over the entire universe, God has always wanted us to experience all of His goodness. That "goodness" is His rest; the place where no labor, sorrow or lack exists. This is the life of God: labor free, stress free and care free. And His master plan is no different for you. Through the practical application of faith, God has given you back that same lifestyle.

I remember once as I waking up early in the morning, I told God how much I loved Him and for some reason I decided ask Him, "How are you doing today?" His response totally shifted my way of thinking and my perspective of who He really is. He responded back gently, "Julian, I'm God!"

Think about that for a moment. You know life is good for God and it should be for you too! I thought, "I guess you're right God, what problems as the Creator and Ruler over all creation, could you possibly have?" His answer: *"None."*

Though the Kingdom message has been wrongly communicated, God wants you to know that He hasn't changed His vision or His plan. He is set in stone toward it and thoroughly committed to making His blueprint your manifested reality. The Kingdom of Heaven is the manifested will of God functioning in every realm of your life. God wants us to truly understand how in agreement He and His thoughts are. He wants you to know His plan for your life hasn't changed.

We have to get this in our hearts. Otherwise we'll keep falling subject to a mentality and life structure our Chief Architect never designed for us. He never mentioned limits, death or sickness when He spoke you into existence. His concept of man consisted of these 3 words: "in my image." He didn't send Christ to change that plan; He sent Him to reactivate it.

Thus He is called the second Adam, retaining all the rights of the first Adam while recovering the ones he lost. When Adam fell, he lost God's blueprint and access to His divine life pattern, a place where the concept of fear, worry and burden are obsolete.

He began to function in a system and paradigm outside of God's nature and intended plan for him. He became aware of another mindset uninspired by God's unlimited existence. Christ didn't die so that you could only experience the benefits of His life after you leave this earth; He died to give you back that life by waking up the God-potential in you. God isn't waiting for you to die for you to experience His blessing!

He already blessed you in Heavenly realms in Christ Jesus (Ephesians 1:1-2) so you could regain access to all His spiritual favor, increase, and prosperity, now! That's why He blessed you. He isn't going to, nor is He waiting to. He already has. If He already blessed you that means there are some incredible things He wants to break forth in your life today.

You have to rise above the common notion that Heaven is a place you only experience after you die. Nowhere does the Bible teach that and nowhere in Jesus' ministry did He teach it either. This is diametrically opposed to God's mind. Traditional thinking has made the benefits of Heaven seemingly unreachable by God's children in this present reality. However, Jesus' core prayer was that Heaven's reality would be produced in the earth, now.

Life now, healing now, peace now, and all of His goodness, now! The truth is you have God's blueprint dwelling in the core of your being. That blueprint is the Kingdom of Heaven: the atmosphere and reality of Heaven living in you now.

So, how can this reality impact yours now? The first step is agreeing and believing that God has already designed a divine pattern for you to succeed. Then you must decide to make His blueprint (ways, thoughts, and principles) the source of life from which you draw. He must become the wellspring of your life, influencing all of your activity from your words to your daily habits.

That is Kingdom culture, the divine influence of Heaven impacting your life causing God's nature to spring forth. Third, you have to become intentional about seeking God's Kingdom so that you may tap into His strategic design to catapult you above every obstacle and barrier and into a dimension of continuous blessings and overflow. Remember that in the Kingdom, what you don't do consistently is the same as you not doing it all the time. Pursue God's intent in your life daily through understanding of the Word, asking and listening.

A Higher Reality

God's design for your life exists to strategically give you the same experience as Christ when He was in the earth, which was a life above every limit. In fact, as His body we are jointly connected to all things; therefore, we are joined to that same limitless life. His plan is for you to enjoy a life short of none of the benefits His Blessing offers. This means that no part of God's richness is to be left out. Whatever you desire you should have; this was Jesus' message. Why is it that Jesus could make such statements? He was living out of the actualization of His ascended place and the present reality of Heaven in His heart. This actualization is the entry point for manifestation and the door that unlocks tangible Kingdom experience.

As Jesus approaches the end of His time on earth, He began to teach the concept of "shalom" to His disciples. He warned them that trouble would come, but in the face of adversity they would have "His peace," leaving them invulnerable to any obstacle they'd encounter. Jesus' concept of peace was not like the peace we know. In fact, Jesus told them "I give you my peace, but not as the world gives."

What did He mean? He was referring to His original plan for man to experience life with no limits, with *nothing missing, broken or left out.* That is the same idea behind salvation, which has commonly been only equated to mean, "rescued from eternal damnation." However, this word stretches beyond that meaning into peace, favor, and prosperity; the richness and the fullness of the Blessing. God's peace refers to the atmosphere of Heaven where everything is added.

See, in Hebrew thinking, Heaven was the only place where true wholeness existed. So you can imagine the reaction of His disciples when He told them "peace" I am leaving the *atmosphere of Heaven* with you or "shalom." Jesus wanted the disciples (and us) to be aware of a higher reality that existed that they had access to through His paradigm, or perception.

The atmosphere of Heaven is the reality of God's presence and the fullness of His grace. This includes healing, overflow, and abundance. All that Heaven's atmosphere has is transferred to us through the Blessing. That is the source of the Blessing, Heaven's atmosphere. That Blessing provides us access into God's supernatural reality, and faith is the extension that links both of our worlds. In essence, the Blessing is the shalom of Heaven; it's God's way of providing us with every solution so that no matter what, nothing in our life is ever missing, broken or left out.

You'll notice in the same message that Jesus taught on shalom (John 14:1, 27), He goes further to encourage the disciples about the problems they would face. He is encouraging them that in this cursed world system, issues will arise because it's a system of poverty and lack. However the shalom of Jesus produces the atmosphere of Heaven, leaving nothing broken or left out in our lives. In other words, He was saying to them, "even when you have a problem, because you have the Blessing, you'll always have a solution."

One of the ways we experience the Blessing is through the abundance of God's treasures, wisdom, and understanding. God has already provided a way out. Shalom is the spirit of un-brokenness, allowing everything in your life to be complete no matter how it may look. The more aware of this completeness we become, the less frustration we will experience in life because God's Blessing adds no sorrow.

Move from Stressing into Blessing

With that said, I truly believe the life of a Christian should be free of the frustrations and exhaustions of life. Many Christians I meet love Jesus but hate their lives. They are tired of their job, they don't like the house they live in or the car they drive; they really wish things were different. They just aren't happy with their present living conditions. This is not God's plan for His family.

Don't get me wrong, I believe what Jesus said when He warned us that we will face problems in this life; however, you have to pay close attention to His words. He has given us His "shalom" (Heaven's atmosphere where nothing is broken or left out). So again, by Him leaving us His peace, He is saying even in the face of what seems to be a problem, you really don't have a problem because the solution already exists. That's why He said, "Take heart (gain confidence through correct perception) for I have already overcome the world." He was referring to a divine strategy and a plan of attack for every scheme of evil. As His body, we participated in the overcoming of the world with Him. We triumphed over the grave as well with Him. We only have to tap into God's divine paradigm and tactics and we'll soon see that we too have already overcome the world.

So, when people become overly fatigued with the perimeters of normal living, something is very wrong. This is called *sorrowful living* and represents traces from the fallen cursed world system that Adam encountered after he was taken out of the Garden. This "world order" shows up in many different forms in our lives. One of the ways is through religious mundane living in which we become so accustomed to the routines of everyday life that we have stopped truly living and lost sight of our destiny, purpose and potential in God. This happens to believers often. As a spiritual performance coach I encounter individuals from all over that are absolutely clueless to God's direction for their life.

For example, it never fails that once people learn about my prophetic gift I get the same type of question most times, "What is God saying about me?" I never make up a word to give people, but I always remind them that the easiest way to know what God is saying and thinking about them is to read His promises and blessings He placed in His Word. Why? Well, most people have no clue about the pre-designed life God has arranged for them. They don't know that He wants every trace of sorrow, lack, and sickness completely eradicated from their life. As I travel the country sharing the good news of God's Kingdom and the Blessing, it's breath-taking to see the way people look at me when I tell them what God thinks about them and expects out of their life. I always ask them, "Why won't you read your Bible?" Typically they are shocked when they learn what the Blessing is and how it can impact them now.

Many people are also shocked when I teach that in the Blessing Christians shouldn't have any problems. Can you believe that? The first time God said this to me, I struggled with it for a long time. I looked at my life and couldn't see how that was true. Over time as I meditated on that truth God showed me, and that principle changed my life forever. You see, Christ is the head and we are His body. That means no matter what we do or wherever we go we are connected to Him and we have divine access to the abundant riches and resources of His Kingdom. That truth is inescapable. You are His body, so everything Jesus has you have too! Christ is the solution. He is the Blessing. He is complete in everything and every way. That means your life is too, even if it doesn't seem that way. The first step is grasping the concept that whatever situations you may be facing today, you don't have to hang your head down or be afraid. You have the solution because you have the Blessing!

The main idea of God transferring His system and all the rights of His Son to us is to give us endless provision. You see, in Eden man is not responsible for His own provision. That was never the plan. God is a King that makes provision for His citizens. However, in the cursed world way of living, man is responsible for his provision; therefore he "sweats and toils" to eat and live. That's why the scripture reminds us that God has supplied all of our needs in Christ. Through Christ, the unlimited provision plan of Eden has been reinitiated and restored. How then can we have any real problems in life? Think about this. A problem would indicate lack of answers or lack of provision. Well, lack comes from that fallen system, the cursed world order. Through God's Blessing the richness and fullness of His resources dwell within us. Anytime we as believers have any kind of problem, it is reflective of a situation that we have failed to turn over to our "head." We can escape every corruption of this world's system by gaining the perception of our "head," who is Christ. Christ is our chief advisor and our eternal headship. He will always show us where the solution rests.

There is no obstacle in your life that God hasn't already seen coming and through His Spirit provided insight, wisdom, and direction for overcoming. For example, if you examine Jesus' ministry He was notorious for always providing a solution. Whether it was paying His and Peter's taxes, multiplying a few loaves of bread and fish, healing the sick, or raising the dead, Christ always had a solution. That's His vision for you as His royal family! That's what the Kingdom of God is: solutions-oriented living.

Our life becomes more compelling the more we are able to tap into God's now promises, which are solutions for everyday life. Answers increase our quality of living. And God, in grace, has lavished upon us all wisdom and understanding to apply His blueprint and live victoriously in every season. This is available to every believer;

however, if you choose to get into worry, fear and anxiousness when adversity presents itself you come from under the Blessing, or the Eden world system, and abort God's provision for you. You must not forget *God has already provided*. His blueprint is a divine scheme to guide us and direct us through life and show us where provision rests. When we tap into this blueprint, He will lead us down paths of righteousness and naturally elevate us above the "gravity of life". That's the power of the Blessing, "It makes rich and adds no sorrow with it!" This includes solutions to any problem that would try to present its face in the lives of God's children. Your job is not to lean to your own understanding and the basic wisdom of this world. You have to connect to the God-life in you.

When you feel the issues of life trying to weigh you down, understand that you aren't subject to those problems. If you receive the message of the Blessing in your heart, then you'll be able to see that every issue of life does truly flow from within us. The Blessing is God's life and the curse is death (fear, insecurity, lack, etc.). The power of that life is in your mouth, and the power of that system of death is also in your tongue. There is nothing in your life that you haven't agreed with consciously or unconsciously through negative words or bad belief systems.

This book will show you that there isn't one problem in your life that Jesus has not already given you a solution for, and through the right philosophies, attitudes and life patterns you can totally destroy every trace of sorrow and negativity from your life for good. You have God's blueprint, the ultimate plan for successful living. You have been crowned with Blessing and restored to righteousness, favor, and honor in the heavenly realms. God has given you His endorsement and has approved your life. You have the crown of life, not just to experience it in Heaven, but because you are a *king* intended to rule in the earth now.

God's plan is still the same. It's a plan to heal you and to heal the land. Don't be consumed with thoughts and ideas of failure and sorrowful thinking as though God may not come through on His Word. Change your perception, open up your mouth and begin to decree out of the unlimited place of God's sovereign kingship into your situations. As the scriptures say *"we have believed therefore we have spoken."* Speak the Blessing of life, favor and increase. Let your circumstances know, "I am not subject to you because I am in God's royal family and I already have the solution." Stand in faith and you'll see God will quickly reveal to you where your solution rests.

It's time for you to experience life without limits and without boundaries! It's time for you to leave a mark in history that can never be erased! Plan for favor and plan to win. You are positioned in the seat of success and one revelation away from your greatest life. You have the power of a breakthrough Blessing that's waiting for you to step into it. Prepare to unleash God's unlimited and supernatural power over your life! Prepare to awaken the sleeping giant and to tap into victorious power paths that will lift you above the spiritual gravity of life's limitations.

Above and Beyond
All Limits I:
The Reality Shift

*"Beloved, I wish **above all things** that you may prosper and be in health, even as your soul prospers."* (3 John 1:2)

Adamnomics: The Plan of Life

Everyday we are confronted with the reality of life's limitations. Daily, we face constant resistance to live outside the box of those ordinary confines. We are taught to think limitedly, and that "we can only go so far." Vehicles are designed and crafted with some of the greatest technology on earth, yet we fail to experience most of their benefits because of laws and restrictions, such as speed *limits*. Think about that: a vehicle can have over 300 horse power and the ability to travel over one hundred miles an hour, but most owners will never experience the full range of its power because they are confined by the law. Often times, this is the case with human potential. We are built for extreme power and speed, but we often go without functioning in the benefits of our full potential because the limits of life have said, "only so far, only so fast." It seems the systems of everyday life have become natural training mechanisms that rehearse within us the mentality to think, operate, and live beneath our God-breathed potential. Your life was created for much more. You, my friend, were never intended to live a normal life.

One of the core strengths to man being created in the image of God was that he was never designed to live within the confines of earth's reality. He was built to live above them. If you carefully read Genesis it's clear that God appointed Adam to manage and have complete dominion over all the systems (kingdoms) of the earth. He was appointed to watch guard, govern, and oversee all of earth's activities and affairs. Adam was the CEO of planet earth. He was responsible for naming all of creation first and placing it in its proper order and place. Nowhere in Eden does a life with limitations exist for man. Eden is a place of dominance, mastery, kingship, and superiority. This is the life you deserve, the power and ability to rule in every dimension of this world. That royal dominion was safely reinvested into you through the power of God's Kingdom.

The Garden of Eden is a reflection of God's intended life for us. If you want to know God's intention for your life on earth, it's easy to find out. Read Genesis chapters 1 and 2. His plan to establish His royal government in the earth realm flows directly from His inspiration to give us a life that reflects His. As the executive officers of the earth realm we are destined to succeed above and beyond every boundary as physical expressions of God's greatness within us. His governmental plan for us is simple: "take dominion over the land!" This same principle remains today. God literally told Adam to dominate. Not just because He wanted to spread His culture, but because of the internal investment of Himself that He had made into Adam's nature.

Since Adam is the first of all living human beings, all humans born after him also come from him, including you and me. That means that

God's previous plan for Adam is exactly the same for you and I; it hasn't changed. So when he told Adam to dominate, He also told us to dominate! A dominator is someone who possesses superiority in any class or field. God's plan for you, as an earthly king, is to give you a life of excellence through His divinely established will. God knows who you are and is sure of what He has put in you. He knows what you're capable of and is confident in your ability to lead your life with excellence.

So God's plan prevailed until Adam decided there was another system (kingdom) better than the one placed on him. He was preyed on by a serpent that was able to convince him that he had not received a system that was superior enough. The simple seeds of doubt and the idea of a life without God were planted in Adam's heart, and from there another "garden" began to grow. You see, it was the seed of one idea that Adam entertained: that he was not superior enough, that he was not made in the likeness of God. Again, by thinking this he became limited. His paradigm shifted and he began to view himself and life through a different lens. Little did he know that God's plan for life was to give him a life in the exact likeness of Himself (by giving him the tools and potential), one in which no boundaries existed. The plan of the enemy prevailed by getting man to accept the lie that he was not like God. The lie of that limitation was the birthing place for the fruit of destruction. It was the cause of the restrictions we now face in a fallen, broken and limited cursed world environment. Through the fall of man, religious lies, logic, and a fear-based mentality entered Adam's world. This made the idea of an unlimited lifestyle obsolete.

As the executive officers of the earth realm we are destined to succeed above and beyond every boundary as physical expressions of God's greatness within us.

> **As the executive officers of the earth realm we are destined to succeed above and beyond every boundary as physical expressions of God's greatness within us.**

The good news for us is that Jesus recovered that Kingdom and reinitiated that original life plan. That means God's plan is still the same. In essence you were never created to live beneath life's limitations, only above them. That was God's vision, and He's still committed to that vision today. In fact, God was so committed to it that He sacrificed His only son (the second Adam) to restore to you the rights of your former self, a life that is now hidden in Christ with His glory.

So what is God really after? What is His big plan? It is to reconnect you with your former destiny! A *you* that isn't fearless or afraid of anything. A *you* that doesn't take "no" for an answer and is no longer limited by the speed limits of life. A *you* that refuses to be denied and is ready to rise above the confines of your present reality. That *you* is hidden deep inside. And with patience, resilience, and unrelenting faith, that same plan can soon be become the reality of your physical existence!

The Law of Gravity: The Cursed World System

Every limitation operates like gravity. It exists to tell you how far you can go and to pull you down. Gravity, being a natural law, does not need permission to exist. It was built into creation and is operating in its assigned function. However, when it encounters God's divine ability it must become subject, as do all other laws that exist, whether spiritual or natural. Nonetheless, the laws and principles of the world's fallen system function exactly the same. They are operating in assignment and are designed to show us what life is like outside of God.

According to Merriam-Webster's dictionary, gravity is defined as the force that pulls and attracts masses to the earth. Picture yourself jumping and reaching as high as you can to grasp your greatest dream. Now imagine every time you jump, the force of gravity pulls you back down to where you began. The cursed world system operates exactly like this. In fact you can think of it as "spiritual gravity". Every time God speaks to us in faith and gives us vision or instructs us to do something beyond our ability we have to "come up" through the law of faith to actually grasp, attain, and see what He's called us to. You'll notice though, that every time you try to "rise" to a place of faith there is a spiritual force working against you to pull you back to where you started. This can come in the form of negative voices from those around us, the insecurity of our own hearts that reminds us of fleshly limitations and discourages us from actually receiving God's promise, as well as the difficulty of our present situations. These factors intensify the spiritual gravity, making God's plan for us begin to seem more and more unattainable.

No matter what we do it seems something is always trying to keep us from believing and fully grasping God's vision for us. We are continually challenged with obstacle after obstacle designed to steal our hope and expectation that what God says about us is possible and achievable. Why is this? Because we are encountering spiritual gravitational pull; a paradigm system intended to operate and function completely against what God desires for us. It's a system, a kingdom with its own practices, laws, philosophies, and beliefs.

God's Kingdom is the direct opposite of that cursed world system and every time you try to elevate above it, its laws kick in just like gravity to tell you it's not possible and remind you of how limited you are. This spiritual gravity is the obstacle to our achievement and can only be overcome by the power that's released through a life that is totally submitted to the government of Heaven.

Now, the cursed world system is designed to operate this way. Again its sole purpose and function is to show you life outside of the Creator. The earthly system, which came into dominance after Adam's fall, is designed and intended to do one thing: limit you! Jesus came to recover and reestablish His government and teach us that once again, the ability to live above these spiritual and physical limitations was now restored to us.

As you examine the life and ministry of Jesus, you'll see it was centered on defying the laws of the earth. He literally defied the laws of gravity by walking on water and disappearing through crowds, proving as the second Adam, all rights of the first Adam had been restored.

You have the right to live above normal limitations. It's okay to expect God to do the incredible and unimaginable in your life. Remember that Jesus wasn't the only one to walk on water, Peter did too!

The Law of Lift: The Blessing Empowerment

When God told Adam to take dominion and rule over the earth, He gave him a divine pattern (image), an empowerment to do so. That system is called the "Blessing." The reason we know that the Blessing is the design and pattern God gave to man to empower him to manifest His image (or pattern) in the earth, is because after He said "Let Us make man in Our *image*" a verse later the scripture says He "blessed him." The Blessing is that pattern, a divine tool, that God gives to individuals in order to empower them to manifest His nature, character, power, and authority in the earth realm. It's God's guaranteed plan for your success and blueprint for living above every obstacle life can throw at you. So every time the laws of the curse say "No, you can't," the superior laws of God's Blessing empower you to respond back "Yes, I can. I am superior to you!"

That's the way God's law works. Kingdom law is the key to living above spiritual gravity and regaining access to the life you deserve. God's law will always tell your situation who is in charge, and everything else around you will yield to it because it is superior law. God has granted you access to this superior lifestyle and through faith you can tap into it! Don't allow the physical perimeters of life to pull you down. Tap into faith and allow God's Blessing to propel you to victory!

God's Blessing is in opposition to Satan's cursed world system (spiritual gravity) and operates much like the law of lift. When the Wright brothers set out on their journey to invent an aircraft there were many naysayers and mockers that told them that they couldn't do it, they were crazy, and how they were bound by the laws of gravity. Resistant to negativity and persistent in their vision, the Wright brothers did not allow the limitations of others to become theirs. They continued to search for a solution, believing that it was possible. They eventually discovered that a superior law of nature called "lift" could overcome gravity.

God's law will always tell your situation who is in charge, and everything else around you will yield to it because it is superior law.

God's law will always tell your situation who is in charge, and everything else around you will yield to it because it is superior law.

Lift, by definition is simply the "the upward force acting on an object." On an airplane, an aircraft wing provides lift by causing air to pass at a higher speed over the wing than below it, resulting in greater pressure below than above. That higher pressure beneath creates an upward force naturally propelling the airplane into the sky. Lift works against gravity in the sense that because the craft is heavier than air, it must use the force of lift to overcome its weight. This weight is caused by gravitational force trying to pull it to the ground. The wind resistance caused by the craft moving through the air is called *drag* and is overcome by propulsive thrust, as well as speed and acceleration. To put it simply, the law of lift literally leverages the pressure of gravity in order to fulfill its assignment.

The Wright brothers didn't have to create a law, nor did they have to deny that the law of gravity existed. They only had to discover a superior law that was already in place. That's the power of the

Kingdom. You only have to discover what already exists inside of you waiting for you to tap into it and rise above every limitation.

The Blessing (Kingdom) works the same way against the gravitational pull of the cursed world laws. The systems of man hinder us and keep us from reaching our potential in God, but God's Blessing is our spiritual lift. We have His divine presence in us to overcome every obstacle in life through Word application. You see, the more that the laws of this fallen world try to deny us our freedom in Christ, the more we realize God's spiritual reality exists. The more we are confronted with negative forces, the more we realize God's superiority is real. It's like the scripture that promises we will mount up as the "wings of eagles." The emphasis is placed on the wings, indicating the function of the wing. The eagle's wing literally creates lift.

That verse is a metaphor describing the limitless ability of God's children to defy the limitations of the earth. Not only that, it describes God's strategic plan to use the negative forces in this world to further propel you into destiny.

What most people don't realize about the eagle is that the eagle flies the highest when the storm is greatest. It leverages the force of the wind to propel it into higher heights. I've got news for you! The more this world tries to limit you, the more they are provoking the unlimited God nature invested into you.

God is using the pressure of your storms to push you into a dimension of your life you've never been. You have the power of lift through God's Kingdom, and the power to dominate without any restrictions or earthly hindrances. You have to remember this in the midst of trial and chaos and begin to speak directly to the storm and tell it *"You're only making me stronger and propelling me to my victory."* God's Blessing is about to lift you above the laws of this reality into the power of His limitless dimension.

More Adamnomics & Conditioning for Eden:
Breaking out of Babylon

It's important to understand that the Bible is primarily written about two kingdoms: the Kingdom of light (God's Kingdom) and the kingdom of darkness (Satan's Kingdom). God's Kingdom is His blessing restored. It's God's life force and pattern given to man to empower him to succeed beyond all limits. That Blessing is life and the potential to win in every season. The "curse" is the kingdom of darkness full of spiritual gravity to contain the greatness in you. We must be aware of this to truly understand the things that take place in our lives. It is imperative we remain conscious that the world is ruled by kingdoms.

The entire message of the Bible is designed to communicate the importance of examining and disciplining your life to ensure that you are living in the right system. Believe it or not, many people are saved and love God but choose to live in a system diametrically opposed to God's ways. How is this possible? Through the principles they let govern their life. It is possible to have the Kingdom paradigm within you, but still function in the "fallen state" or paradigm of Adam. That paradigm determines the kingdom that rules your life.

When Adam was taken out of Eden, the place he was put in was a "spiritual Babylon." You'll notice through the Old Testament that Babylon was the most powerful city to emerge. It was the capital city of Persia and the wealthiest place in the country. This city was also a practical expression of the kingdom of darkness and its authentic rule in the world.

Among other benefits, Adam mainly lost control over his environment and the divine ability to think like God. God's greatest gift to Adam was that He had given him His mind, the righteous ability to think and imagine without limits. When Adam fell from that state of being, he saw himself as "naked." That nakedness is a picture concept used to express the illustration and idea that Adam was now aware of his limitations. So what this passage is really communicating is that Adam was now able to imagine or see limitations; therefore, he was now subject to them. His mindset had changed and it had become limited or "fallen". This fallen mindset is what we are born with in the earth realm. It's a mindset that causes us to focus on our limited ability only and not see beyond the flesh into the unlimited power of God's divine nature within us.

As long as Adam was naked he could only focus on himself and his own limitations. In fact, if you examine chapter 3 of Genesis closely you will realize that God never changed how He dealt with Adam after his fall. God Himself came down in the cool of the day to have regular fellowship with Adam as any other time. However, something was unusual this particular day. God could not find Adam. He was hidden from God in a place that God uniquely designed for him. This is the system of Babylon. It impacts the way we see ourselves, which in turn influences how we see God.

God, determined to commune with Adam, went on a search until He found him. Now, let me just point out something significant: if God *found* Adam, that means Adam never came out of hiding. God searched for him until He located him. (This is a spiritual principle that all Christians must keep in their hearts. God is hungry to fellowship with us and His love and compassion drives Him to keep seeking after us even when we don't want to be found.) Notice Adam's response to God was that he hid because he was naked and afraid. Let's just take those two concepts right there. *Naked*, as mentioned earlier, is used to represent limitations or a limited self-picture. *Afraid* means he had fear.

Fear here, is more than a deep worry or anticipation of harm, but it also includes all of the characteristics that came into Adam as a result of his new fallen mindset. Fear expresses insecurity, doubt, and impoverished thinking. All these can be summed up in one word: sorrow. Sorrow is the source of the spiritual reality of the curse. It means at this point Adam had lost all capability of completely trusting

God and walking in faith. He did not trust God's way of doing things anymore because the sorrowful mentality had overcome him.

Our own insecurities and limitations may change how we see God, but they have never changed how God sees us.

> Our own insecurities and limitations may change how we see God, but they have never changed how God sees us.

Now that Adam was no longer doing things God's way, he became subject to a mindset that made him more and more insecure about his connection to God. Yet, God covered him with a robe of righteousness even in the midst of his rebellion. Our own insecurities and limitations may change how we see God, but they have never changed how God sees us. In His eyes, He still wants the same thing for us that He has always desired from the beginning: to be like Him. That's difficult in a world that is full of godlessness and voices of godless chatter, but you have to be resilient in your faith, choosing to defy the gravitations of life no matter what people say, think, or how they see you.

In essence, Adam had changed kingdoms. He was no longer living in the Blessing, but now he had become subject to Babylon and its limited way of thinking. This mindset is like a city or place that is built by the walls of philosophy, ideas, and belief systems. Our mindsets are living structures that become spiritual homes we live out of. The idea that Adam was taken out of Eden and placed in another city clearly displays what really occurred with the fall. Although the Garden of Eden is a real place, it's also a detailed expression used to communicate to us the concept of life before man's fall. Adam was in a spiritual place while living in the physical realm. Adam, like you and I, was functioning out of two realities. Though he was in the earth he was thinking on a level much higher than it. In other words, when Adam fell from his divine nature he lost those elevated thoughts, concepts, and philosophies. It was like someone being taken from their home and being placed in a totally inferior environment.

It's important to understand that as Genesis accounts the creation of the earth, it doesn't account for the creation of Eden. To this day, Bible experts have been able to trace every historically documented place in the Bible back to a physical location except for the city of Eden. That's because Eden is a spiritual place. It's a real city that Adam was conscious of while living in the earth. This spiritual city had so much physical impact it caused a Garden (city) to spring forth in the middle of an environment full of chaos. That spiritual city is the Kingdom of Heaven. This city has been restored to us with the same ability to bring the spiritual place of Heaven into physical manifestation once again in the earth. We have the Kingdom in our hearts and the divine ability to tap into its unlimited impact through our faith. I want you to ask yourself, "What city have I been living out of?"

Adam was no common man, that's for sure. He lived a life that superseded the limitations of the earth because God created him superior to it. Man was made outside of the box of creation; therefore, we have the divine right to live beyond its physical boundaries. Ideas and philosophies are the building blocks of our spiritual city. The Bible is clear that Adam was taken out of the Garden and placed back into the place from which he was taken. That place he was taken out of is the earth, the place God pre-designed to plant man to influence with His glory and nature. This ground was a place where no grass, trees, or fruit had sprung forth. Again, this is a visual image communicating the present state of the Babylonian mindset.

Earth was the place Satan had been cast into after his fall from Heaven. From the time of his fall to the formation of the man, Satan had been working and trying to design his own world order independent of the Creator. When it says no grass had sprung up, it's really telling us about the principles and philosophies of spiritual Babylon. They don't produce favorable conditions. It's the idea that the concepts of this world were fruitless, dry, and impoverished. This was the concept Satan had been working on since his fall. His intention was to create a whole new world outside of God where he could be king and ruler. He was only able to produce thorns and thistles, and the ground was cursed. That's his system of principles and ideas, a life outside of God.

These ideas are the patterns and architecture of the spiritual city of Babylon. It's a living arrangement that trains and teaches individuals to live a lifestyle independent of knowledge of their Creator and His way of doing things. This is the dominant concept in the earth right now. Man often thinks contrarily to God's unlimited laws. Why? Because, they can't see beyond the limitations or overcome the gravitational pull of the cursed world mentality. It's because of this system, along with its laws and principles, that Christians are unable to experience the unlimited tangible reality of the Kingdom lifestyle.

Most Christians that have the Kingdom within them still choose to live in the spiritual city of Babylon. They build with its walls (principles), streets (ways) and orders. Babylon is systematic and it trains them to think beneath their divine potential. Babylon comes from the word *babil*, which means to jumble or confuse. Babylon is the spirit of sorrow that fosters sickness, labor, and unpleasant living conditions; it confuses the purpose of God in your life. The goal of the Kingdom is for you to experience heaven while still in the earth realm, just like Adam. Yes, God's plan is still the same.

You cannot be neutral. You are either living under the Blessing or you're still functioning within Babylon.

You cannot be neutral. You are either living under the Blessing or you're still functioning within Babylon.

What you must understand about these two realities is you cannot be neutral. You are either living under the Blessing or you're still functioning within Babylon. The curse operates through fundamental philosophy of carnal thinking and sin. When I say carnal don't just equate that to the fleshly indulgences like sexual immorality. By carnal I am referring to an earthly mindset. A way of thinking that just limits your perspective on life and says you can only do so much. It makes you overly conscious of time and puts brackets on your faith and ability to trust God when He doesn't move between certain time frames. It teaches you to think poor, speak poor, and live poor. Poverty is not the lack of money; it's a condition of the heart. Lack of money is just one of the manifestations of a poverty mindset.

Many Christians are afraid of prosperity, succeeding, and advancing beyond all odds. They are afraid to be great because of the impoverished mentality of Babylon that has taught them not to expect great things out of their lives. Spiritual gravity continues to say to them, "You'll never be more than you are today. You've reached your limits and there isn't anymore God can do with you." But God is never finished with your life. You haven't even begun to perceive the incredible things He has in store for you once you break out of the box of life. Things can change in an instant if you will allow God to breathe within you His fresh breath of unlimited life, health, and prosperity. Let Him pump you full of His thoughts and belief systems. Gravity is no match for the spiritual laws of God's Kingdom within you. You have the God-given ability to tap in to a supernatural city not made by hands that defies every negative weight and mindset this world has tried to place on you. Let the Kingdom impact your life now.

Throughout the Bible we learn how the systems of man can easily influence our thinking and cause us to miss out on the supernatural reality of the Kingdom. As spiritual aviators we must not allow gravity to pull us down to its limited level. The transition from one house to another, or from one city to the next, takes place in your asking. You have to ask God to show you how to live in His spiritual city once again. Tell God that you desire His way of life and His way of doing things. Tell Him to give you a reality shift!

When a reality shift happens, our minds begin to become free from all the hindrances of cursed world thinking and renewed to a spiritual paradigm of Heaven. You can feel yourself breaking free from every hindrance of Babylon as you begin to change your words, expectations, and concentration to the reality of the Kingdom. The spiritual city of Eden is ready to impact your world now. New rivers are about to spring forth in your life. Jesus promised us that if we drink from Him we would flow with the abundance of rivers. Those rivers He is referring to go back to the four rivers in Eden (Genesis 2:10). Jesus was trying to say that Eden was inside of us and once again its abundance is going to overtake us.

Imagine your life full of the abundant flow of Heaven. The rivers are inside of you waiting to be unleashed. God has promised to restore Eden through His Blessing, which came upon us through Jesus once again. It's our eternal right, as royal sons of Heaven, to obtain that elevated lifestyle once again. You deserve it! Not because of anything you did, but because of the love of God and Christ's triumphal feat over the cross. Here are some of God's promises to restore the city of Eden within you:

> [*The LORD will surely comfort Zion and will look with compassion on all her ruins; he will make her deserts like Eden, her wastelands like the garden of the LORD. Joy and gladness will be found in her, thanksgiving and the sound of singing*] (Isaiah 51:3).

> [*They will say, "This land that was laid waste has become like the Garden of Eden; the cities that were lying in ruins, desolate and destroyed, are now fortified and inhabited"*] (Ezekiel 36:35).

> [*Eden Restored*] *Then the angel showed me the river of the water of life, as clear as crystal, flowing from the throne of God and of the Lamb*] (Revelation 22:1).

As we unleash Heaven within us we will see our realities shift according to the unlimited nature of our King. Peter experienced this reality shift in Luke 5:4-7.

> *[And when he had finished speaking, he said to Simon, "Put out into the deep and let down your nets for a catch." And Simon answered, "Master, we toiled all night and took nothing! But at your word I will let down the nets." And when they had done this, they enclosed a large number of fish, and their nets were breaking. They signaled to their partners in the other boat to come and help them. And they came and filled both the boats, so that they began to sink.]*

Notice in this passage the word Peter used to describe the business was *toil*. Toil is the same word for *sorrow* in the Hebrew, meaning labor, sweat, fear, poverty, etc. Remember that toil and hardship came into Adam's life as a result of his fall and introduction into the cursed world system. So what's happening here is Peter's business is trapped within the laws of a spiritual Babylonian paradigm and its operation. Although he's a capable fisherman, he can't seem to get over the hump in his fishing business. This is because he still is being governed by cursed world mentalities, principles, and words. Peter is confessing that he *can't* catch any fish, and as result he is subject to that reality.

However, when Jesus (the Blessing) enters the boat he becomes subject to another system, the Kingdom of God. He tells Jesus "at your word," which is God's spiritual law. Peter literally told Jesus, "At your law I will stop saying what I have been saying and I will listen to you." Peter allowed a new law and system to govern his reality. He changed kingdoms in an instant and within minutes he was making the greatest catch of his life.

What happened? When Peter came into the reality of the Blessing, he shifted and the limitations of time fell off. In God's Kingdom the brackets of time are irrelevant. Thus, what Peter toiled for all day and night in the curse was reconciled in a few minutes in the Blessing.

There are no limits in Eden and you have every right to draw from its endless supply. This is called breaking out of Babylon and creating a reality shift. This is done by influencing three main cultural blocks. Essentially Peter was able to change these three core areas of cultural influence and the impact was immediate:

1. *Source*: who and what we trust in
2. *Language*: how we communicate with God and others
3. *Philosophy*: what we think and how we view life

How Limitations Operate

The book of Daniel (1:1-5) teaches how Babylon trains and how an entire culture can be influenced with source, language, and philosophy. Limitations exist through these areas. If you can break free in each one, you will gradually begin to see the limits falls off.

> *[And when the king returned to Babylonia, he put these things in the temple of his own god. One day the king ordered Ashpenaz, his highest palace official, to choose some young men from the royal family of Judah and from other leading Jewish families. The king said, "They must be healthy, handsome, smart, wise, educated, and fit to serve in the royal palace. Teach them how to speak and write our language and give them the same food and wine that I am served. Train them for three years, and then they can become court officials." Daniel 1:3-5]*

Language:
Breaking Language Barriers

Everything God speaks to us, whether in His Word, personally, or through revelation, emerges from a position of pure faith. Until individuals function completely by faith it will be difficult to truly grasp the things God has promised them. All wisdom and understanding of God's Kingdom is found in the one He raised from the dead (Colossians 2:3). This is referring to faith teaching. You can't believe in Jesus Christ unless you believe He was raised from the dead. So the only way to truly access the complete understanding of Christ's Kingship is through faith.

Nothing God ever says is based on the reality we live out of.

Nothing God ever says is based on the reality we live out of. Whenever God gives us vision or a message, it's completely spoken out of a realm solely governed by the laws of faith. God needs us to understand this. You may notice most of the things God tells you to do, whether through His Word or by revelation, are always beyond your natural ability. That's because where God lives, nothing is impossible and the confines of time, spiritual gravity, and human logic are irrelevant. God is not talking to the fallen you, He is actually speaking to the Christ in you. Many Christians fail to understand this principle, and as a result they experience great frustration when trying to regularly communicate with God. Often times they end up confused and unsure about His direction for their life.

As a traveling speaker, I commonly encounter Christians frustrated in their relationship with God because they don't have a clear understanding of what He is after in their lives. This frustration has led to a bad belief system in the church that God doesn't speak to people every day. I've noticed that when it comes to communicating with God most Christians don't believe God desires to speak to them.

They think prayer is them talking to God only. Well, neither is true, and God is not a respecter of persons. He doesn't say to one "I'll speak to you" and to the other "I don't want to talk her." That isn't it at all. Hearing and communicating with God is performing spiritual law just like any other function in the Kingdom of Heaven. And when you come into a Kingdom paradigm shift, prayer becomes a matter of God talking to you versus you just talking to God.

You are in a relationship with the King, a spiritual King at that. So being prepared to use your faith whenever you are dealing with Him is imperative. Like all relationships, a relationship with God requires some form of constant and unhindered communication in order to succeed. One of the most difficult things to do is to operate in a relationship where you are constantly misunderstood, so God's purpose for communication must be greater. It's impossible to build a healthy connection that way. These types of relationships have what are called *language barriers*.

Many Christians today have great language and communication barriers with God because Babylon is still influencing how they speak. They fail to realize God is a King who functions by spiritual law. He is also a Spirit who requires faith at all times to interact with Him. Some people don't even believe that God desires to deal with them intimately and constantly even though the scripture is clear how much He loves us and is always thinking about us. We can't afford to think this way. We have to know that everyday God is waiting to speak to us, tell us something, give us an assignment, and hear about the things that are on our hearts.

In this Kingdom the King desires to have a personal relationship with all of His citizens. People often talk about how high above our thoughts God's mind is. This scripture is quoted a lot, but it is usually misinterpreted as if God never can nor does He want to ever be understood.

Why would Jesus go through all He went through on Calvary to make you a part of His royal family just so He could never talk to you? Does that make sense? Like I said earlier, it's a difficult thing to be in a relationship with someone who constantly misunderstands you. Things just can't work that way.

Communication is the heartbeat of any relationship, and God expects daily and constant communication with us. He certainly doesn't want to be misunderstood. What is meant by that verse is that God functions opposite our way of thinking, but He doesn't want it to stay that way!

On the contrary, the same mind in Christ is in you (Philippians 2:5)! This is precisely why Colossians 3:2 commands us to think like Christ, setting our thoughts above the earth. He doesn't ask us to, He commands us to. Why? Because we have already been given the nature of God through Christ when we received His Holy Spirit.

All of the DNA and life of Christ have been deposited into every believer. This means we have the ability to understand God and commune with Him on a daily basis. He has so much to tell us and is excited to get His unlimited treasures over to us through wisdom and knowledge.

All of the DNA and life of Christ have been deposited into every believer. This means we have the natural ability to understand God and commune with Him on a daily basis.

This wisdom gives power to discern how to apply His Word every day to ensure the Kingdom is always in active perpetuation in our lives. As long as language barriers exist we can never truly become who God ordained for us to be, because we haven't communicated correctly with the One who made us.

All of the DNA and life of Christ have been deposited into every believer. This means we have the natural ability to understand God and commune with Him on a daily basis.

The Law of Asking

Breaking those language barriers begins with consistency in the Word and prayer. A keen focus must be applied to conversing with the Holy Spirit, who comes to communicate the will of God to us and teach us all of His ways. When we pray, we have to routinely ask for wisdom and understanding. At the same time we must remain aware of the constant obstacles we face through language barriers and consistently attacking them with the Word and revelation.

I need you to understand that when I say *ask* I don't mean to beg. I am referring to the dimension in which Jesus taught us to pray. That's through putting a constant demand on God through confidence in His Word. We have a right to speak to God and be in His presence (Romans 5:1-2), not by anything we've done, but by the spilled blood of Jesus on the cross.

The ability to fully grasp the idea that communing with the King is a royal right given to the citizens of Heaven will determine the quality of one's prayer life. Praying isn't simply telling God what we want and then desperately hoping He'll do it. This is the way most people pray and it's out of alignment with the scripture. Prayer is law, and one of the principles of prayer is asking.

Asking in the Kingdom is a different concept than asking in Babylon. It means we adhere to what God has said about us and already done for us in His Word, and by applying faith we place a demand on God for its manifestation. This is proper communication with God for two reasons. 1) It's law. Prayer, like any other Kingdom concept is a law. It's God's institution of communication that gives us direct access to Him and all of His resources. This also gives God the right as a Spirit to intervene in human affairs. 2) It's done in faith. The law of prayer and the law of asking are related, but not quite the same thing. The law of prayer establishes the different forms of communication we can have with God. The law of asking is simply one of the ways we place a demand on God for what we know He has done. This, however, can be operated several different ways. When we ask, we are supposed ask as kings ask, which is formally placing a demand on what we know that the King has already stored up for us. Notice with the Lord's prayer, Jesus said pray "this way." He didn't tell us to pray the same words over and over. He simply gave us a model for effective prayer.

The most important part to this prayer is that Jesus never begs or pleads for anything. He always tells God what He wants done. That's asking in a Kingdom. This doesn't bother God at all, nor does it cause us to appear arrogant in His eyes. It's actually an expression of our confidence in His promises. Just like kings speak to other kings, God expects us to come with boldness before His throne (Hebrews 4:16).

A perfect example of this is Jesus at the fig tree with His disciples. Jesus was confident in the laws of faith, prayer, and asking. He simply approached the tree and stated His demands. Then He left. The next day the tree was uprooted as He commanded it. What's interesting is He told the disciples if they tap into faith they could do this with a mountain! What? Now most people, though limited mentalities find it difficult to grasp or see how this is even logical. First of all it is not logic, it is faith. Faith specializes in the impossible. It breaks limitations.

Notice how Jesus never repeated Himself after speaking to the tree, and the most important part, He walked away. Why did Jesus do this even though He didn't see any results from what He said? Jesus was able to walk away because He knew the law of faith was already functioning on its own. He didn't stay to see what would happen because He had already received it by faith, and He understood it was pure law working in its established order. Jesus had no doubt that tree would be uprooted because of His understanding of how to communicate through law. All of creation was built in with law and is governed by law. It functions in a system with orders, classes and principles.

Creation is also aware of who created the laws that govern and established it. In the beginning God, out of faith, began to speak what He could not see physically. Genesis 1:1-3 lets us know that although He created the earth, it was formless and void. Which means the creation they are referring to had formerly taken place in His mind. This is powerful, because we cannot place a demand on God for what we don't know is already ours.

When Jesus spoke to that tree, His confidence provided such a rest that He could leave and come back. Now again, it's important that when the disciples inquired of Him how to do this He explained to them that as long as they have faith they could do the same thing with a mountain! Think about this. Jesus literally told them "if you can tap into the law of faith, whatever you ask for has to do the same thing you saw with this tree." Why? Because it's law, it's invariable and unchanging and has to operate the same way regardless of the situation.

Now, here is where the law of asking is presented. Jesus said whatever we ask for (place a demand on) in prayer we have already received it. Meaning, you are justified by faith and no one will have to tell you that you've received something from God. Once you have truly asked in alignment with faith, you'll know it and you'll receive it!

Once you've received it, you can speak what you know you already have. It doesn't matter what it is. The law of asking works for anything. This is the point He is trying to get across to them. Nothing is impossible with God when you tap into His divine laws. Ask and you will receive it! You can almost sense the passion of Jesus in this particular verse, because the core of Christian living is right here. To rephrase His statement: "If you tap into the law of faith, there will be no limitations on your life. You can demand whatever you want and you will have it and see it manifest in your life."

Nothing is impossible with God when you tap into His divine laws. Ask and you will receive it!

This all comes down to the fact that through applying God's law, you can break every limitation off of your life. Since God's law is the highest law

Nothing is impossible with God when you tap into His divine laws. Ask and you will receive it!

operating in the earth, by breaking into it we can live out of Heaven's unlimited resources in the earth. Breaking those communication barriers will establish a better understanding of God's Word so that you can better communicate with Him. As a result, His direction for your life will be clear and you will be able to walk in the limitless possibilities God originally intended for you. This includes defying every limit that manmade philosophy has ever tried to place on you.

Ask (acknowledge what God has done first). Seek (receive it by faith). Knock (place a demand on it). When you change your language, you change systems and begin communicating out of your elevated nature. When you speak the right language, God's law has permission to function properly in your life.

Source:
Learn to Live by Faith Alone

The concept of living out of the faith realm totally transformed me and shifted my reality. It changed how I view life and how I see my own. I began to search God's mind for other laws, and by gradually increasing in His Kingdom I began to view life's matters through His lens, or perspective, and no longer through mine. This changed everything because in God's mind no limitations exist. There are no confines to His vision or His imagination. Once I began to take off the blinders of the world system it became more and more clear to me what God was after in my life through His government. I began to realize that I had the option of living life solely out of my own vision or that I could walk in God's vision too. In Genesis 9, after the flood, God told Noah to walk blameless, upright, and to walk "before" Him. I soon learned that what God meant by "before Him," was "in His sight," implying *His vision*. He simply told Noah, "Walk in my original vision for you." God's original intention and vision is the best plan for our lives and His will is to get the lifestyle He envisioned over to us through faith.

Once while learning the laws of faith and how to tap into them God gently spoke this phrase to me: "Faith is not the key, living by faith alone is." I was confused at first, but then He came to me again and said, "The main ingredient to faith living is your total dependency and trust on its power to always come through." Then I remembered what Paul said in Romans 1:17: *[The righteous will live by faith alone.]*

It wasn't until God began to deal strongly with me about this concept of faith alone that I realized the most important word here is "alone." (Some translations leave that word "alone" out, but this is the original way it was written.) This means I'm not righteous, or all rights of the King aren't translated to me, until I grasp the concept of "faith alone." It's only when we learn to trust in God's Word [law] alone and make the decision to cut out all other options and sources for living that faith comes alive. If I want to operate above the systems of this world, I cannot rely on them or be connected to them in any form or fashion. This includes my language, thoughts, and behaviors. It means choosing to rely on God's Word alone, even in the face of adversity.

For many believers, faith isn't their only choice. When things don't seem to be working as they expected they begin to yield certain areas of their lives to the earth's system by speaking out of faith, worrying, and entertaining fear. When they do this they grant access to the laws of sin, sickness, poverty, and lack.

Living by faith alone cancels any other options. This means that as I follow God I am willing to take the next step, even when I cannot see the next two. When this happens people step completely out of earthly limits and outside of themselves. They are putting total force on the law of faith and allowing Heaven to manifest itself completely and unhindered in their situation. Until I have decided that faith is my only option, I cannot live in faith; therefore, faith cannot work for me nor can I live out of my "Heavenly Dimension."

Living by faith alone cancels any other options. This means that as I follow God I am willing to take the next step, even when I cannot see the next two.

> Living by faith alone cancels any other options. This means that as I follow God I am willing to take the next step, even when I cannot see the next two.

Here are nine practical truths about living by faith that can activate its full force in your everyday life:

1. Faith must be viewed as an unfailing law that works every single time, and only when you use it all the time.
2. Faith has no limits.
3. Faith cannot be simply viewed as a means to get things from God when we want something. Although this is one of its functions, operating solely based upon that concept of faith will cause major frustration for those who try to tap into it. This type of perspective does not encourage repetition in the Word; it promotes only stepping into faith when you have a need.
4. Faith should be seen as a person, not just a concept. He lives in you through Christ by the indwelling of the Holy Spirit. As long as you acknowledge faith, it will acknowledge you.
5. You have to keep faith at the forefront of everyday living. Everything you do must be done in faith. Only then are you justifiable. That means made righteous, or in right standing with God's law (Romans 10:10). This "righteousness" places you in the perfect position to access all the resources the Kingdom has.

6. You must choose to operate completely by faith. Until then you are not in complete alignment with God's highest law. This is one of the main reasons people struggle to release the Blessing. The Blessing of Abraham came through faith alone, that's it. Until individuals learn to live by this principle, the Blessing remains undisclosed to them.

7. Only when you live by faith do you access the rest of the laws that exist in God's Kingdom.

8. Living by faith alone requires more than reading or even just declaring the Word. Reading and declaring God's Word are important elements as well, but the core ingredient to functioning in the faith realm is operating in a mature wisdom and understanding of the Word of God. I'm telling you, it begins right here. Colossians 2:3:

   > [. . . *in whom are hidden all the treasures of wisdom and knowledge.*]

9. If we must believe Christ was raised from the dead in order to believe in Him, then faith is the main proponent for accessing His wisdom. Through that wisdom we learn how to operate the Kingdom of Heaven with skill.

Thought Life: Learn to Think Above the Earth

As a renewed creature and citizen of God's all-inclusive Kingdom, you have the legal authority to supersede any human or demonic system with ideas and thoughts that flow from the unlimited space of God's imagination. Our thought life is an important cultural block that determines the overall pattern of our thinking. If this cursed world system can successfully influence your thought patterns with ideas and models that resemble the basic patterns of this world (Colossians 2:3) you will once again be subject to bondage and mental captivity.

This does not mean that you have not been fully redeemed from the curse, or the fallen paradigm, of Adam. However, it is important that you realize the only way to become subject to that fallen nature again is to take in fear-based philosophies that are constantly being impressed upon us everyday through a number of outlets. Remember that in Daniel 1, it was imperative that the literature, or brain food, that Israel's men took in was totally Babylonian-inspired. A change in our thoughts and mindset is guaranteed to change our words and language system. How we communicate in this world and with God will certainly determine the overall impact we are able to have for God's Kingdom in the earth.

In this book we will look at some principles of super charging your thoughts and modeling your thoughts after the design and pattern of our King, Jesus Christ.

2

Above and Beyond
All Limits II:
Unleashing Heaven's
Atmosphere

"The "Kingdom of Heaven" is a condition of the heart . . ."

-Friedrich Nietzsche

Creating a Kingdom Paradigm

I n order to experience the reality God has intended for you to live in, you must understand and grab ahold of the meaning of an expected end (Jeremiah 29:11). That expected end is His will, purpose and intent for creating you to dominate in this earth. It is the destiny that is lying within you and waiting to be unleashed. Jesus didn't come to talk about religion. He came on a political campaign. His message was about living in a new type of government and experiencing all of the benefits of its reality now. His message was not just about recovering, but about reawakening the greatness in you that God invested before the creation of the world in the intimacy of His infinite imagination. Jesus' purpose for coming to earth is a mirror reflection of God's intention for creating you. It was to make you aware of the actual existence of His nature still in you lying dormant waiting for you to place a demand on it. In other words, Jesus came to wake up the sleeping giant within.

Within you is that unlimited investment, the ability to influence your life with the nature and authority of the supreme Creator. If you're going to experience life with no limits you need to understand where you came from. You need to shift your mentality about who you are and why you're here. You need a clear understanding of why Jesus came so you can know what it is that mankind lost when Adam fell. By regaining this awareness you can tap into the limitless grace within, the internal kingship of Christ, who is waiting to rule from the governing seat of your heart. This is called creating a Kingdom paradigm.

Jesus only preached a Kingdom, because that's what was given to man in the beginning. However, that Kingdom is not just a regimented system of laws and orders; it is a concept and a way of life. The Kingdom of Heaven is a superior world view that takes on the perspective of God and empowers you to live out of His paradigm. In fact, the Kingdom of Heaven is a spiritual paradigm that governs the thoughts, ideas and perspectives of an individual's life.

It's within your grasp. It always has been. This is why Jesus preached it this way: "the Kingdom is at hand." Again, He means it's within your grasp, just like it has always been. But now it is time for you to awaken that God-paradigm that can cause you to emerge as the unlimited divine being you really are in the world. This means the Kingdom's ability to influence and impact one's life is dependent upon one's awareness that this Kingdom actually exists. One must actualize the Kingdom in order to place demands on it and draw from its unlimited resources.

This explains why He taught, "Repent, for the Kingdom of Heaven is at hand." *Repent* is "metanoya" in Greek, meaning to change one's way of thinking or to shift paradigms. That is the first access point of manifesting the Kingdom lifestyle. You must take on the reality of God's perceptions, and you must have a paradigm shift. When you realize the existence of Christ's complete and unhindered authority within, the Kingdom comes alive in you.

The Blueprint Concept

My Blueprint Theory suggests that deep within the nature of every creature lies the inherent source and hidden capacity to produce the same qualities, characteristics, capabilities, and creative genius of its maker. In the Kingdom this means every person, by the reactive source of the Spirit, can produce the same behaviors and overall lifestyle of the King. This lifestyle is called the Kingdom culture, the ability to reproduce the nature of God with divine influence in every sphere of our world.

Each culture has its own source from which it derives. It produces inherent characteristics of its source, called DNA. Spiritually speaking, the term DNA is the root cause for all spiritual order that manifests in both Heavenly and satanic systems. In order to produce any culture, the inheritor must possess the same qualities as the hereditary giver, making it possible to express that same nature in a tangible life form. In other words, the essence of Kingdom culture is the inherent spiritual DNA of God being reproduced in the earth through us His royal family as a tangible expression for others to see.

The Kingdom operates in reproductive cycles. Its nature is to create offspring of the King (mature sons), reproducing His nature and His likeness with the purpose of spreading and impacting the nature of everything else it touches. This is called Kingdom influence. When the spiritual DNA of God is successfully deposited or downloaded into the life it touches, the natural genius of God will begin to emerge in that person as a reproductive force and cycle. That DNA of God at its very core represents the science of God's mind. It is His creative genius, analytical ability, and most of all His innate governing strategy. Though all things created do not glorify Him or acknowledge Him as source, He is still the sole Creator of all existence.

Kingdoms play a major role in the collective system of life. Everything can be categorized into an order, species, genre, and class. The list goes on concerning categories and classes of species such as plants, animals and humans about how they function in their respective kingdoms and environments. Those kingdoms represent a system that groups species with like natures and characteristics, ranking from the lowest to the most superior kind.

This is called order, and in our case would be referred to as the Kingdom order. So, how do orders operate? Simply by systems put in place to create harmonious arrangements of parts working together to produce a particular society or culture called a "whole". If you haven't realized it by now, God's plan through His shalom and Blessing is for you to be completely whole, enjoying life to the fullest. That same wholeness flows from God's DNA that He perfectly invested into Adam before the fall. It creates a perfect picture of God's rest in our mind that by relentless pursuit can overtake the physical reality we experience. It's also a sign that we have reinitiated an open Heaven within us as a regular flow and outpouring of God's supernatural grace and strength beginning to influence and take over our lives. That's God's purpose of investing His DNA into man, so that His life would "flow easy" within us.

So you see, every system has its order and every order possesses its own culture. And the Kingdom order comes to divinely impact and influence the humanistic systems of the earth with the divine culture and DNA of God.

A Heavenly Invasion

The core driving point behind God's Kingdom coming to earth is a principle called "Kingdom advancement." Kingdom advancement is the ability to spread, influence, and govern any environment with its culture and systems. Consequently, the Kingdom of God has no limits or boundaries that exist because it is inherent of its Creator, God, who is the limitless King.

What this means for us today is that just like its King, the Kingdom infiltrates through government authority by way of concepts and principles designed to produce the overall lifestyle of the Garden. You and I literally get to reclaim the lifestyle and the provision package of Eden by shifting into the paradigm of our God nature within. When this happens we invite an invasion of Heavenly influence and its benefits into our environments. As we continue to grow in this revelation, all doors will open and blessings will flow to us easier when the complete system of Heaven has been successfully downloaded into the atmospheric environment of our existence. This is what I like to call a "Heavenly invasion."

In order to experience an authentic invasion of Heaven, we as Heaven's citizens must understand how things "in Heaven" operate. First we need to recognize the Kingdom is filled with God's DNA and this means the mind of God is the source of the King, the place from which the spiritual DNA of God derives. His creative DNA rests in us all as hidden potential waiting to be reawakened to consciousness. In fact, we were created with His spiritual DNA, which gives us permission to act, speak, function, and build our lives from the design God has so generously endowed us with through His Blessing.

Awakening the Sleeping Giant

It's plain to see that God wanted to reproduce Himself in the man. No man can gain real purpose or destiny without the resurrection of the life of God within him, his DNA. It is important to realize that the nature of God resting in you has been frustrated, or made subject to the will of Adam. Within in us all is the will of Adam, God's first offspring, created in the image and likeness of the Creator. Naturally, as Adam is the firstborn of God's creation, we all then become inherent descendants of Adam, subject to the same DNA and order of our progenitor.

This means when God sees the entire population of man, He only sees a "kind" of man. He sees Adam. We too became subject to the decisions Adam made since we are his offspring and we follow in his order and design.

Whatever government Adam lost, we lost. Whatever system he chose to live in, we live in. It is the law of generational code, the offspring is influenced by the actions of its progenitor, and so by nature we have the same qualities, actions, and characteristics of Adam. The same quality of life Adam possessed before he fell, we too possess the same hidden capacity to experience that lifestyle. So even though Adam was created and designed with God-life in him, the fall caused it to go to sleep. In the same token we are born with God's unlimited life force asleep or at rest in us. However, we must undo the frustration of the will of Adam that has forced the DNA of God in us to be dormant and under constraint.

By the public confession and declaration of Adam, he had chosen another system by which he would operate and design his life with. He was no longer subject to the will of God, simply because he and God were functioning in two separate paradigms and lifestyles. This was Adam's decision and God, who gave Adam free will, honored it.

Adam left God's pattern for what seemed to be a better one. After all, he was like God, powerful and capable to do anything he wanted, so why should he subject all that power and authority to someone else? In essence, this was the question posed by the contender of God's Kingdom, Satan.

His purpose and intent was to get Adam to believe that God was withholding certain information from him that could give him a better lifestyle than the one he already had. His challenge to Adam was that God was "holding out," and trying to keep him subject so that he couldn't experience life on His level.

In other words, "there is another system (tree) you don't know about, and if you will just eat its fruit (concepts, principles, and philosophies) you will be in a superior class and become like God so you don't have to be subject to anyone's authority."

Just like trees grow from "root systems," the tree represents a particular system, or as we discussed earlier, a kingdom order. Remember a system is made up of integral parts working to maintain a particular whole (i.e. culture and society).

So, the fruit then becomes what produces the mindset, characteristics, and culture of that system. Remember now, that kingdom impact successfully operates by establishing itself through reproduction, which in this case would be the concepts and ideas of its source.

So imagine Adam and this tree (which represents an opposing kingdom). Day after day, he is going to begin eating along with his wife, taking in new concepts, philosophies, and principles. Daily his mindset is changing along with his perspective of how he sees himself and life. Simply stated, Adam had a "new paradigm." Next his behaviors follow as the digestive evidence of his change in thought process and vocabulary set in. He is changing everything, his culture, mentality, and belief system. He is taking on the inherent traits of that system's source, who is Satan, the king of this opposing reality.

Now the blueprint is laid, the pattern is developed and Adam is going to start operating out of a totally different reality than the one he was placed in based on those characteristics he's producing inspired by the concepts and mentalities he's taken in. So notice very carefully, God comes to visit Adam and is unable to find him. Why? Well this is a Garden, or sphere, ruled by the concepts and philosophies (DNA) of God. It is no longer "home" to Adam, because he no longer holds the same belief system as God. So in essence he is like a foreigner.

It is important to point out that Adam lived in east Eden where God placed him. East Eden was the only place the Garden was growing at that point. Adam then, would have been either west, north, or south, where the philosophies of God had been planted but not yet cultivated in the earth.

When God finally locates Adam and asks what's going on, his response is "I hid, because I was naked and afraid." Now, pause there. I want to point out again that this is the first place you see words of fear and limitation appear in the existence of man's creation. These are words never used by God. All through the creation of earth and Eden God never used this type of vocabulary. Why? Because fear and limitation are not apart of His DNA.

Adam's words are flowing from his source and the culture he has now adopted as his living structure. The society Adam has now become apart of is full of fear and sorrow. Adam is demonstrating this new nature when he says he is naked and afraid.

As stated above, the word nakedness means "limitation." Up until this point Adam could look down and only see the limitless (no seams) and creative nature of God. Now he looks down and sees his "own" limited nature. His perception of who he is has completely changed and he is operating out of a "fallen paradigm." Therefore, the Kingdom paradigm has gone asleep within him. When he uses the word fear, it is going to represent more than an expectation of harm. Rather it is a Hebraic reference point to illustrate a child that is alone that has become disconnected from his parents. He is then afraid, hopeless and without identity.

Here, with this particular phraseology, Adam is illustrating his position as now being "separate" from God in nature, ideas, and philosophies. By acknowledging his nakedness he publicly declares he and God are no longer "together" but now he is on his own and afraid. In other words, "we no longer think the same; therefore we are not the same." That is why God couldn't find Adam. They were functioning in two different dimensions now.

Now that the God-life in Adam is going to sleep, he is going to fully take on this new paradigm of fear-based living based on the principles he has inherited through interaction with this tree (system).

At this point man is banished from Eden and placed into the cursed world system where the mentalities they have now taken on rule. The limited concepts and philosophies Adam has now adopted are illustrated by the thorns and thistles he encounters outside of Eden. This makes clear the unfruitfulness of this system.

It is the same darkness referred to in Genesis 1. Darkness represents the fallen concepts and ideas that were governing that area of earth. Those ideas are the inherent traits and characteristics that designed that society. Every person who lives in this fallen society is limited and bound by the perceptions of its fallen paradigm.

Now, for the first time in Adam's life he is a limited thinker. He cannot rise above the ceiling of his thoughts. This paradigm haunts mankind today and causes him to struggle with grasping the concept of who God really created them to be. Many people have this fallen paradigm about a business God called them to start. They struggle with this complex about a ministry God has given them a vision for. Why? The fallen paradigm of Adam has limited their thoughts, making it difficult to rise above and tap into faith and endless vision

So how do we escape this fallen paradigm? First you must understand that when Jesus died on the cross he broke Adam's contract with death and became that fallen world system so that you could break free from its paradigm and experience unlimited life (Galatians 3). Secondly, you must understand that now, you are the only one who can contain the greatness in you. Unless you reawaken the Kingdom paradigm you'll always have an inferior complex about something big God has called you to do.

Notice in Romans 8:20 that creation is subject to frustration, not of its own choice, but of the will of the one who frustrated it. There is only one answer to releasing frustration out of your finances, relationships, health, and emotions: you must release the God nature within by awakening and unleashing your God-life through revelation knowledge. You need to align your heart with God's paradigm so that you can unleash an unlimited flow of Heaven's reality. You need to release a Heavenly Invasion.

You see, Romans 8:20-23 explains that creation is not crying out for God. Why not? Because God didn't frustrate it with His will, Adam did. So the earth moans for the sons of God, the original God thinkers who operate in the image, pattern, or spiritual DNA of God. (Remember that spiritual DNA represents concepts and principles.)

The only person who can remove the frustration or "cursed world system" from creation and your life is Adam, the original son of God. However, since you are made in Adam's image, God is talking about you!

God cannot remove the frustration of anything in your life as long as your will is in the way. Remember that your will in your own life will always be more powerful than God's will in your life. You are the only one who can take up Adam's mantle to reproduce God's Kingdom culture by faith and revelation. You must awaken the sleeping giant that's in you. Then at your will, God will do whatever you ask of Him.

Your will in your own life will always be more powerful than God's will in your life.

Your will in your own life will always be more powerful than God's will in your life.

God's plan is to unleash Heaven for you by strategically influencing your will with His ultimate will so that His intended lifestyle for you can become your reality. Remember that the Kingdom of Heaven is the manifested will and intentions of God flowing in every realm of your life. You have to learn how to "conform" so that God's will becomes the source that generates your thoughts, life, and decisions.

The way that you allow God's will to transform your life is through a process called "spiritual adaptation." In this process the Kingdom is made clear, actualized, and materialized.

The Kingdom Process: Spiritual Adaptation

Now, there are three levels to spiritual adaptation, which completes the Kingdom process. 1) *Internalize*—the point at which information is new and beginning conception. 2) *Formulize*—the point at which constant and consistent repetition creates persuasion and familiarity. At this stage ownership of certain truths emerges and your mind begins to conform to God's mind. 3) *Materialize*—the point at which ownership reaches a level of finesse and high subconscious activity. It is usually evident in some tangible form. This is where the principle begins to materialize and takes over one's reality.

Every core driving point of culture we examine requires this 3 level process in order for us to successfully "own" a spiritual principle or truth. In the Kingdom, you can only manifest what you are, nothing else. This is the mindset and law of "I am."

You are what you have become through certain downloads of information. That is the Hebraic concept of being: *you are (I am) what you believe and what you believe is what you are*. In other words, what you are attracting into your life is a result of things you believe deep down inside, causing that paradigm to manifest through words, behaviors, and decisions.

All of this encompasses your will, because everything we think, do, and decide flow from our free will. This is very important to understand, because in Hebrew, your will is who you are. It's the most powerful thing you possess as a physical and spiritual being.

It is the source of your paradigm and consequently the source from which you attract things in your life.

You see, the term "I will" doesn't exist in Hebrew language, only "I am." The future tense is wrapped up in the present tense, because in their way of thinking the future already is. In fact, the word "future" in Hebraic concept is likening to a man rowing a boat up the river of life. However, he is not looking forward to the future, in this concept, he is rowing backwards into the future while looking back on his present. This simply means your future is actually behind you, or it already is. The present however, is what's in front of you. So, this is why you can't say, "I will" in Hebrew, because what you have planned or willed to do, you've already become that thing. Instead, you can say "I am going to the mall," or "I am going to grab a bite to eat," etc. Again you can only say I am, because you are what you have willed to do. This is how God thinks. It is His culture given to the Hebrews. Furthermore, the idea of *will* as we know it is also covenant or contract in Hebrew.

There are two ways to see the English word "will" in Hebrew: "now" and "covenant or agreement". To add further credence to this point, the words decide & declare are actually the same words in Hebrew as well (to decide is to think or judge), because what you've said is also you have decided and what you have decided is your will. In other words you are what you think or decide. Jesus put it this way, *"As a man thinks in his heart so he is."* Notice, in this verse the concept of "I am" is established when Jesus says "he is." Why did Jesus say this? Because this is how God thinks; this is His perspective of who you are. You are what you think, will, or decide.

If this is God's paradigm, that means spiritual law is established based on this understanding and concept of "I am" and your will. In other words, spiritual laws respond to your will, not your words only. You must will what you say. So, when Adam said, "I am" naked, God was forced to honor his confession because it was his will.

So, what do you really believe? Because it is that will the universe is honoring in your life, not just what you say. It is that will that shapes your paradigm and that paradigm is responsible for drawing and attracting the people, places, and things that are in your life.

This brings us back to the point that all three levels of adaptation are necessary to fully adopt a Kingdom truth and put it into active manifestation. You must become the truth you desire to tangibly manifest. In other words you must will it, become it, and say it. Then you will attract it.

You must will it, become it, and say it. Then you will attract it.

Referring back to Daniel 1, we see that spiritual adaptation exists to ensure that you

> **You must will it, become it, and say it. Then you will attract it.**

"become," or rather you are "immersed," in any truth, idea or culture you are in so that you can successfully manifest and reproduce it. Because remember in the Kingdom you don't attract what you want, you only attract what you are.

So, whatever misconceptions flow from your paradigm you are attracting into your life, be it spiritually, financially, relationally, etc. You will only attract the things you will deep inside, which means we cannot prosper in the Kingdom *until our souls prosper* (1 John 1). The soul is the place of will, emotion, and thought.

The purpose of Kingdom adaptation is to take you through a series of spiritual metamorphosis that totally changes your inherent spiritual DNA, awakening the core belief systems of God so that you may unlock a steady flow of Heaven's atmosphere in your life and begin to attract everything like God to you. Remember the Kingdom comes so that God's will is done, to manifest in every area of your life. So if you can unleash God's will in your life, you will attract things that reflect His will. This is the power of Kingdom manifestation, releasing the will of God as your power source.

As you are unleashing the Kingdom of God within you, the good things you say and declare will come to pass, and out of the good treasures (paradigms and belief systems) of your heart you will bring forth or "attract" good things!

The Human Energy Field

Over 75 trillion cells make up the entire existence of the human body. Much like that of a battery, each cell possesses electrical properties and electric potential. Those electrons and electrical forces play an intricate role in our everyday life and existence. In fact, they are as important to us as the air we take in and the water we drink.

Think about that. You are one big electricity field creating and releasing tangible energy that determines the overall function, health, quality, and natural state of your body. Quite simply put, you are one big ball of tangible energy.

Whether you realize it or not, there is an invisible flow of electrons encompassing the entire earth. Though this is not popularly known, it is very important to understand this invisible energy force that lies over the earth's surface. Furthermore, this natural flow of electrons and its related energy field also exists on the surface of all conductive objects (including people, plants, and animals) in physical contact with the earth.

The natural pulsating voltage of earth is impactful in several different ways. One is that prior to mankind wearing shoes it allowed them the benefit from direct physical contact with the earth. As a result, the human body naturally connected to and maintained the earth's voltage on the surface of the skin, throughout the respiratory system, and in gastrointestinal functions and tracts (which are conductive).

An interesting fact is that as mankind has evolved into a modern society, for instance in the area of shoes, they have lost that connection with the earth. It is scientifically proven that shoes cut off that connection between the earth and the body. Consequently it's less likely that the human body will reside under the protective umbrella of the earth's direct current electric field. Again, the human is an energy field. It has long been known that activities of cells and tissues generate electrical fields that can be detected on the skin surface.

However, the laws of physics demand that any electrical current generates a corresponding magnetic field in the surrounding space. At first these fields were thought not to be of significance by scientists due to their microscopic size that made them very hard to detect. However, it is now a widely accepted truth amongst biologists and physiologists the effects these magnetic fields possess.

Subsequently, it has been discovered that all tissues and organs produce specific magnetic pulsations, which have become known as bio-magnetic fields. Quite simply, everything we do is fueled by electrical signals running through our bodies.

Remember that everything is made up of atoms, and atoms are made up of protons, neutrons, and electrons. Protons have a positive charge while neutrons have a neutral charge, and electrons possess a negative charge. Out of balance, these charges determine whether an atom is negatively or positively charged. This switch in charges allows electrons to flow from one atom to another. This flow of electrons, or a negative charge, is what we call electricity. Considering that our bodies are huge capsules of atoms, we have the ability to generate massive amounts of energy at any given time.

Consider the nervous system and how it sends "signals" to the brain, or how the brain tells you to put one foot in front of the other as you walk. This one of the most basic examples of electric currents being sent from point A to point B. It's no different than digital cable signals carrying 1s and 0s that deliver the visual of your favorite TV show. The only contrast in our bodies is electrons aren't flowing along a wire; instead, an electrical charge is jumping from one cell to another until it reaches its destination. You could say electricity is a key to our survival.

When God blew breath, or His life, into man, it sent an electrical impulse and current within him, generating a new life form and making him an element of the highest energy. Man is designed to function by the operation and signaling of electrical currents.

Electrical signals are fast. As a result we are able to transmit instantaneous messages within. Our bodies do not rely solely on the passing of chemicals. If they did then when the message to tell hearts to speed up when something is chasing us needed to be sent, we probably would've died out a long time ago.

Those crucial signals that tell our hearts to speed up when we're in danger are simply electrical currents passing at the speed of light. Just like our heart, any part of our body is capable of passing an electrical current and charge. In fact at this very moment your brain is sending electrical charges as you read, comprehend, and understand this passage.

Supercharge Your Atmosphere

What does this mean to you? Human beings are made up of energy. That's what we are. However, this energy doesn't begin in our physical body; it starts with our spirit man, our souls, and then our bodies. Let's look at how our spiritual energy can help create and shape the environment needed to escape chaos and produce conducive and healthy living conditions for success.

In Genesis we find that the world and all creation including humans sprang forth from the life-giving energy of God's Word. The moment God said let there be light His tangible energy was released in the earth giving all creation the ability to produce magnetic energy fields of their own. In fact, John 1 refers to the Word as light, which is simply energy. As energetic beings we have flowing through us positive and negative protons that are creating invisible fields we live under.

Our sphere of influence or "garden" is made up of this energy, whether negative or positive. Whatever we release in our thoughts and words literally create energy fields that will draw things to us based on the energy we exude and release. The positive energy flows from the Kingdom of God, God's nature, and His blueprint in us.

The negative energy flows from the fallen nature in every man. We have the ability to choose what field we will live in based on our words, philosophies, and the relationships we entertain. This field will determine our destiny, as the energy of who we are will ultimately release and attract to us what we have invested into our outer spheres.

A good example is when Elijah prayed for rain (1 Kings 18). He was charging the atmosphere, waiting for a release because it was due. It was simple supernatural law, he created a field or cloud of tension and the discharge was due because of his simultaneous declarations.

The "Garden" is a spiritual atmosphere created when the right things are continually spoken into the right place. God consistently, for seven days, spoke into one spot in the earth and created a magnetic field with a supercharged atmosphere called "Eden." The Kingdom of Heaven is a spiritual diameter and an invisible magnet that is only effective if we are charging it with the right things. That's why whatever you sow comes right back to you. Your field is generating a discharge. If you say I'm sick of my job enough times, you'll get sick or you'll notice conflict emerging with the boss and now more and more problems arise, because you kept charging your atmosphere with those atoms.

In the same way, when the right principles are spoken into the right place they will eventually make room for new energy. When this happens a discharge occurs and draws exactly to you the charges you have released through thoughts and words.

A discharge is a release of tension and energy. We see this with lightning and thunder. Once the stress or tension of energy in the sky reaches a breaking point, the clouds release a discharge in the physical form of lighting and the audible sound of thunder. This is what God is after He appears in the Bible in a "cloud" of Glory and thunder and lightning are surrounding Him. These are all illustrations and displays of how His Kingdom operates.

What do you say the most? That's what is happening to you. Faith is the "substance" of what is hoped for. That means its material substance is produced by an expectation for something. "Sub" means under, and "stance" means to stand. It's literally standing ground; that's an atmosphere or reality. You are creating the ground you walk on and the reality you live in with your words.

So if your faith is the spiritual substance of what your expecting, your words become that spiritual substance causing that thing to tangibly take form through the energy of words being released into the atmosphere.

When you put a seed in the ground a crop grows. Easy. As long as it is cultivated and properly watered it will produce a crop. That's your atmosphere. When you speak words you sow into your future and what you have said will soon enough discharge and a harvest will come forth. If you declare, "I am wealthy" enough it doesn't necessarily mean money will appear in your lap the next day. However you will release ideas and strategies that can make you wealthy because that is what you've sown into your atmosphere.

All of the characteristics, qualities, habits, and connections you need to become wealthy will begin to flow to you because of the discharge you have created in your spiritual Garden. If you are willing to apply those strategies and take action, you will inevitably begin tapping into your wealthy place.

Words have real electromagnetic power and substance so they create waves, sound, frequency and matter. The question is what are you charging your life with?

What's in Your Atmosphere?

Many people have created negative fields. They have believed a negative concept, idea, or philosophy for so long they've created a spiritual field that only yields that harvest. We confess but see no results. We declare but we don't see what we have said. Why? It isn't because you don't possess the God-given potential to produce it. It's because some of us have created huge spiritual fields that can only be broken by the power of the right words being constantly spoken in the atmosphere.

We have to change our atmosphere by changing our words; however, changing our words and speaking the right things continually takes commitment, discipline, and follow through.

We have to change our atmosphere by changing our words; however, changing our words and speaking the right things continually takes commitment, discipline, and follow through.

For so long I struggled with depression and a pessimistic view of life. I couldn't seem to get ahead and it seemed like doors were always closing on me. I used to think to myself "man I sure have the worst luck." Actually I was right! As a result that's what kept on producing in my life and atmosphere.

> We have to change our atmosphere by changing our words; however, changing our words and speaking the right things continually takes commitment, discipline, and follow through.

My breakthrough came when I decided just maybe how I am thinking and speaking could be influencing this perpetual negative cycle. So I decided to change my thoughts and my words. For 90 days straight I focused on disciplining healthy, positive, life-generating thoughts and positively charged words. I decided it was my life and no one was responsible for it but me and I have the power to change things.

I quickly noticed that when I changed my perception about certain things, right along with it followed the kind of confession I was making. I began to see that things in my life were exactly how I said they were because I believed it. Therefore what I believed I became.

That's any energy field created by thoughts, imaginations, and words. I had to break that negative field I caused through deceptive mentalities and negative fear-filled words. In some cases I had to make the right confession for 60 to 90 days straight in order to see breakthrough in particular areas of my life. Many of us have said things for so long that the words we use aren't powerful enough to break that atmosphere immediately.

You have to choose to say the right things consistently and consecutively, around the clock, owning your day with supercharged and faith-filled words. Doing this will eventually begin to move out those negative electrons in your atmosphere you need in order to experience and attract God's best for you. I believe the Kingdom of Heaven itself shows up as an intangible energy field and force that when yielded to will produce the reality of God's most favorable conditions in your life.

Apostle Paul briefly shared about this experience by saying that if we keep our minds above the earth, Heaven's atmosphere will explode into our physical reality (Colossians 3). He encouraged us that our minds are the meeting grounds for the birthing of God's reality.

He also reminded us that if we aren't thinking about higher things we aren't going to produce higher things. He promoted "elevated thinking." However, if we keep thinking on and speaking positively about our future, that old climate will eventually break and a shift will take place producing a supercharged atmosphere for breakthrough, miracles, and open doors to discharge and overtake our realities.

So, many of us just need to keep saying the right things and eventually they will show up. Realize though, that in some cases you are breaking a negative field and eventually the right atmosphere will emerge and discharge to you the electrical current of your words. If we have been declaring something and it seems that it's not showing up, it may not be our confession but our atmosphere.

Sometimes we need to change what's in the atmosphere before we throw out our faith. If we throw out faith in a negatively charged field, it will paralyze our words. So begin taking authority over the atmosphere of your money, relationships, and body. Step into mental peak performance by disciplining your thoughts to change the energy of your spiritual umbrella. Speak and decree, "My atmosphere is changing." Begin to declare, "I recharge the atmosphere over my finances, body, relationships, and life."

Break up that fallow ground, shift the field and dismantle negative forces. You can expect things to change, as new clouds will begin to emerge and store up the good things you've been saying. Soon, there will be a discharge of opportunity and great doors are going to open up for you because you are deciding your destiny with the atmosphere you are creating.

Breaking Contracts

Many times negative energy wants to take over your atmosphere and invades your thoughts with faithless unbelieving statements and words. You may hear negative things trying to cause you to began speaking them, about yourself, and drawing them into your atmosphere.

The truth of the matter is nothing anyone says to you has the power to come to pass unless you agree with it. One of the ways Kingdoms function is by the law of agreement. It simply says: *nothing can take shape in my life unless I've agreed with it in some shape, form or fashion.*

Many of us have made contracts with negative forces because we believed the wrong principles. What we have to do is break those contracts with our words. We have to disagree with what's been said. We have to say something different or else what was said will continue lingering in our future and governing our realities.

I remember once when one of our staff members had come down with gall bladder disease, but was healed by applying this same principle. She realized that she had been creating the right atmosphere for what the doctor and others had been saying to produce by not cutting off their words. During one of our leadership trainings, I taught on this concept of "breaking contracts" and "changing your atmosphere". She grabbed ahold to the principles and began to apply them on the way home. One of her confessions was "I disagree with gall bladder disease and every negative word that has been spoken. I do not agree with you."

After that it was inevitable. Her atmosphere changed and her new words began to take root. Within seven days of her confessing the Word she was completely healed! What about you? What have you been saying for so long about a particular thing? Maybe it's time to break the contract, sever the ties with those faithless words, and give permission for something new to break forth in your atmosphere.

Take time to examine and acknowledge things that you may have released into your atmosphere that would sabotage your future. Flee from gossip, stop slandering, and commit to subjecting your tongue to words of life, peace, and prosperity. I've learned that when negativity about others is released from our mouths we only spew venom and poison into our midst that will eventually come back and bear fruit in our own lives.

Be sure to examine your heart, forgive others, and speak blessings over them, not curses. In that way you will continually be speaking life and supercharging your environment with good things. You will build up a tangible release of God's favor and power in your life.

You have the power to change your atmosphere. Take authority and begin causing your spiritual climate to shift. Right now you can begin attracting good things to you with life giving words of faith, favor, and increase.

3

Supernatural Living I: Living out Kingdom Law

"Through Christ Jesus the law of life has set me free from the law of death." (Romans 8:2)

The Attitude of Possession

Since we are now a part of God's royal family in Christ, joined together with everything in Heaven and earth (Colossians 3:16-20, Ephesians 1:10), we are then naturally partakers of God's richness and abundant supply. This means regardless of what it is, whether in Heaven or in earth, God has given us direct access to it by His favor. We as "His body" and we can be confident in the abundant Kingdom lifestyle knowing that there is no part of God's unlimited Blessing that He ever wants to keep from me and you. If you think about it that would contradict the purpose of joining us to Him along with everything else. There is nothing missing in His plan to bless us; not one thing has been left out.

Sometimes believers become discouraged in their relationship with God. They often wonder if God is withholding blessings from them or if they are being chastised for something in their past because they lack results with His Kingdom. They feel as though it just isn't working for them.

The reality is there is nothing God wants to keep from His royal family. I've heard this taught in the church for years as though God picks and chooses which of His children He wants to bless more based on something they've done. This is far from the truth. The idea that God is trying to keep any one of His children from any part of their divine inheritance is completely opposite of what His Word promises.

Now, the concept of maturity is a requirement for living in your total inheritance. However, you must also understand that the type of maturity God requires is simply a seasoned understanding of revelation concerning His Word.

When a believer comes to the maturity (or fullness) of wisdom concerning any Kingdom law and learns to practically apply it, God then does not become responsible for its perpetuation in their life, they do. Remember, God's responsibility as maker was putting His spiritual law in place; the responsibility to take action on it is upon us. In order to get real results with the Kingdom it is imperative that we as royal citizens get it down in our hearts that everything God is ever going to do for us, He has already done. He's already given us all things by joining us to His Son, Jesus.

Not only that, but He accomplished all of this before the creation of the world. So, since we have been "redeemed" or restored to our original state of being, why then would God keep anything from us now that He planned to give to us since the beginning of creation? I want you to really think about this: everything God desired for you since the beginning He desires that same thing for your life now! Though you cannot see it, it's been hidden deep within you and God has freely given you everything He has given Jesus because you are *"joined together with him."* Look at this passage in Romans 8:32:

[He who did not spare His own son but gave him up for us all, how will he not also along with him, graciously give us all things?]

Here we see plainly that God has given us "all" things and having done so, He has already accomplished everything He is going to do. You should get excited about this. That's why God rested on the 7th day of creation; there was nothing left for Him to do! He had already put in place every gift, promise, blessing, and solution to every problem you will ever face. Why is it then, that believers struggle so hard to tap into what God has so "graciously and freely" given them? Why do Christians find it difficult to experience the Blessing in a tangible manifestation? The answer comes down to a simple spiritual principle called "Law."

As Christ is our Head we must understand that in Him exist all of the principles and sciences of God. We as His [governing] body are called to live out of our Head while in the earth. That means leveraging His spiritual law in order to live above the limitations of the earth's systems. It is a must for believers to learn how to function in spiritual law, especially if they desire to experience real transformation, walk in dominion, and have a lasting impact for Christ in the earth.

I've noticed that most Christians today have a difficult time trying to influence other people's lives with the Kingdom. They want to be Kingdom establishers but have no real understanding of what the Kingdom is, its laws, or how they function. As a result, when people look at the average Christian's life it looks about the same as theirs.

The Kingdom is a divine impact on human and satanic systems that cause the unlimited purpose and manifested will of God to emerge in every sphere of our reality. This means "normal" should not be in a Christian's vocabulary. Our "light," or Heavenly influence, should be so visible that people know that we are functioning in a world separate from them.

The Kingdom is a divine impact on human and satanic systems that causes the unlimited purpose and manifested will of God to emerge in every sphere of our reality.

> The Kingdom is a divine impact on human and satanic systems that causes the unlimited purpose and manifested will of God to emerge in every sphere of our reality.

Yet, in some cases, people can look at a Christian's life and genuinely feel they are better off where they are in their own. How is this possible? There has been no real transference of Heaven's reality into the life of most Christians because they have failed to release its tangible power through actualization of Heaven's existence in them. This leads to a lack of proper application of supernatural law.

When people fail to "realize" their Kingdom potential, all that God has invested in them lies dormant because they aren't continuously seeking out the God nature within them. Think about this: *If we are sick, impoverished, fearful and frustrated, don't we look exactly like those living in the cursed world system?* What's left to entice them to give God's system a chance? This is what makes the application of supernatural law so important. When God's supernatural Kingdom is properly applied, Kingdom law can eradicate every trace of cursed world principles from anyone's life! Remember that the *"Kingdom is not a matter of words, rather it is a matter power and demonstration."* (1Corinthians 4:20) People will always be more influenced by what they see rather then what they hear.

This means Kingdom influence is not measured by flattery words or how much we "talk" about what God is doing for us. It is measured by our ability to manifest Christ's complete unhindered government along with His entire spiritual law system in a tangible expression for others to see. Remember that Jesus said, *"the Kingdom is within you."* (Luke 17:21). Since the Kingdom is spiritual and it exists inside of us, then an inward alignment and full conceptualization of how its spiritual laws operate is required in order to produce outward manifestation.

See, once the fullness of God's Kingdom has impacted our life internally, it will naturally begin to leak out into our physical reality spreading to every sphere of our existence (finances, family, health, relationships) causing them to align with the reality of Heaven.

Every law and governing principle of Christ is strategically established and designed to propel you beyond the basic limitations of this world. This is called "living out of your Head." Again, as Christ's body, our life's assignment is taking on the mind of Christ (the place where God's abundance exists) through His perfect law, releasing the atmosphere of Heaven for us to live out of.

Again, in this atmosphere nothing is broken or left out (shalom). It is the pinnacle of living and it produces the life you deserve every time its principles are applied. Every time you tap into Kingdom law, you tap into Heaven's governing power causing you to release a greater dimension of its reality in your personal life.

Supernatural Power

Tapping into the Kingdom life isn't easy. If it were, then everyone would be living in it. In actuality many believers are saved, have the Kingdom, but are not living out of its reality. Truthfully it can be a struggle grasping spiritual concepts and getting God's entire system to work and function freely in our physical lives.

The main issue believers are facing when it comes to experiencing the Blessing is actually grasping the Kingdom concept and actualizing the reality of Heaven's present and existent rule *within* them. They also struggle to live in the Kingdom because it cannot be seen with the human eye nor can it be perceived with any of the five senses; it's a spiritual Kingdom. However, we must not forget that this spiritual

Kingdom is designed and intended to have a physical impact in our physical reality.

As I mentioned previously, the Kingdom is the Blessing restored, and it releases not only the material blessings of Abraham, but also the spiritual blessings of Christ (Ephesians 1:1-2). It's a spiritual paradigm, that when awakened in us exchanges a fallen conceptual worldview for an unlimited worldview.

It is important to understand that the Blessing has two parts to it: the Abrahamic side and the Messianic side. The Abrahamic side is the physical/material part. The Messianic (Christ) side is the spiritual part. In essence, Jesus' sacrifice brings both sides back together to restore back to mankind the complete fullness of the Blessing Adam was endowed with before the fall. It awakens the pre-fall Adamic paradigm lying dormant in every human being. This Blessing not only includes total access to the eternal riches of Heaven, but also access to living out its material substance in the earth. To further bring light to this concept let's briefly examine the "Melchizedek Order" found in Genesis 14:18-20:

> *[Then Melchizedek king of Salem brought out bread and wine. He was priest of God Most High, and he blessed Abram, saying, "Blessed be Abram by God Most High, Creator of heaven and earth. And praise be to God Most High, who delivered your enemies into your hand." Then Abram gave him a tenth of everything.]*

The name Melchizedek is actually two words in the Hebrew. It means *Malki*—"king," and *tzedek*—"peace." Thus you have the common expression of his name, the "the king of peace." Now, we understand that peace in the Hebrew goes back to the meaning *"shalom,"* which is nothing broken, nothing missing or left out. That is why he is also the "king of Salem" (shalom), as in Jeru*salem*. "Peace" then can be substituted for the word "Blessing." So you could also read his name as *"the king of Blessing."* Now, before any of this takes place Abraham is still waiting on God's promise that He would *"bless him."*

Though it is commonly misunderstood that at this point Abraham is walking in the Blessing, he is not. The possessions and goods that Abraham had accumulated prior to His defeat of Kedorlaomer and the other kings by lying about Sarah being his wife for fear of the Egyptians killing them both. After this, Pharaoh gave him increase "for Sarah's sake." Lying and fear are both traces of the cursed world system. Furthermore, if God had already Blessed Abraham there would have been absolutely no need for his encounter and meeting with Melchizedek. So it says Melchizedek "blessed" Abraham, and it was at that point he received the fulfillment of God's promise to bless him.

This is important because Melchizedek was both king and "priest of the Most High God." The king part represents earthly dominion, while the priest part represents spiritual dominion. Notice then, that he "blessed" Abraham by offering him *bread* and *wine*. Again the same concept applies: the bread represents the earth and the wine represents the realm of the spirit. This is the two-sided or "double portion" blessing that Adam lost: authority to reign in the Heavenly realm and authority to reign in the earth realm.

So Abraham received a double portion of blessing; 1) *the bread*—material blessing and 2) *the wine*—spiritual blessing. Although he received both sides, Abraham is only going to be able to demonstrate the material side, because both parts of the blessing, including the spiritual covenant, could not be released until Christ would come. This is because Jesus is the perfect sacrifice that restores back all that man has lost through the Adamic fall. So notice throughout the Old Testament you'll see that Abraham's promises always had to do with land, houses, prosperity (gold and silver), and physical well being. This is because he is the father of the "material blessing." Yes, God has made a covenant to increase you materially while in this earth. Never forget that.

Christ, however, comes in the same likeness of Melchizedek, inviting His disciples at the Last Supper to partake in an offering with Him of bread and wine. He told them that what they were doing and the power of what it represented was going to be fulfilled only in the Kingdom of God. (Luke 22:14-19) This was because Christ, through His death and resurrection, was getting ready to recover, restore, and release upon man both sides of the entire Blessing once again. The fullness of that Blessing is on you. When you joined and became heirs with Christ, the bread (material blessing) and the wine (spiritual blessing) found fulfillment in *you* through the Kingdom. You are now a legal royal heir and adopted son with complete access to God's unlimited system through revelation and realization of His unlimited paradigm.

The most important of all this is the immediate action Abraham took to ensure possession and manifestation of this system. Lets look at what Abraham did to activate this enormous Blessing that had just been placed on his life. He applied spiritual law through this principle: *"He gave a tenth of everything"* (verse 20). Abraham understood that in order to possess and activate this Heavenly system just given to him he had to apply some type of law (take action). Now, it is very important to note that the literary work and historical studies of Jewish scholars confirm and describe that the tithe Abraham presented was not the standard tithe described in the Torah as given on an annual basis, but was of the form of a one-time "tribute offering." Abraham's intent in doing so was to establish and express that God sustains his entire world through His Blessing and Favor and that (tribute) tithe-gift merits God's Blessing of monetary wealth. Again, there is a covenant with you to prosper you materially in the earth.

Giving is just one way to tap into spiritual law; however, when we operate in this principle we make the declaration that our life is not governed or ruled by money and earthly systems, rather we are saying that it is ruled by the Kingdom and that God is our sustainer and provider. It is then up to us to bring our own lives and every dimension thereof back into submission to God's Blessing so that everything we have may also become subject to and influenced by this unlimited empowerment. What I am saying is, supernatural law is waiting to impact your life. However, you have to become aware that it exists inside of you, tap into it and apply constant force to it in order to experience its power and unlimited benefits. You don't have to let the unlimited system of Heaven lie dormant in you anymore. Make the commitment to actualize the Kingdom within you, and to reawakening this double portion of inheritance you gained through faith in Christ. Receive the Kingdom paradigm and allow God's reality to reshape your perspective and expectation of life.

Activating Kingdom Law

By nature every law, whether natural or spiritual, must have some type of pressure or force applied to it in order for it to function. There is no law that exists that operates without pressure being applied. That's one principle of operating in law: it must have force applied to it. The Kingdom is the most revolutionary concept and force in the world today. Yet, we have allowed this revolutionary concept to lie concrete because we've been uneducated and unintentional about learning how to live in it. The Kingdom is for everyone and possesses the power to radically change your entire reality with a little force and consistency being applied to it.

Keep that word at the front of your mind for now, *force*! Force is one of the ways law is activated. You have to understand that at its core, law is simply dormant potential waiting to be tapped into to fulfill its function. Let's take an example. We can draw from Newton's 1st law of motion as it best describes this function of force. It states: "every object will remain at rest or in uniform motion unless opposite force is applied to change its state." This means a law is at rest until pressure has been applied to it. This same principle is constant even in our daily life. You see, you cannot benefit from the purpose of any object or device without first applying the correct force to it. For instance, let's take something simple like a remote control and my HD flat screen television. Now, the remote is law, and so is my television. Both have been built and configured to operate a certain way every time they're used, as long as they have been activated and function properly.

Now, in order for me to experience even the most basic benefits of having an HD television, proper force must to be applied to the start up button in order to turn it on. From there I have to know what button controls can get me to the HD stations so that I may enjoy the enhancements of HD programming. (Just a side note: The first time I bought an HD flat screen I didn't know how to access HD channels. I didn't feel like reading any instructions so I went frustrated for almost 3 months. So, even though I had the benefits of an HD television along with HD programming, I couldn't enjoy any of the features because I lacked training and proper application.) So it's quite simple, I apply the correct force to the remote and I get access to my HD television and all of the HD programming I desire to watch. The remote, the television, and the programming all have been designed to perform specific tasks that when brought together, through applied force, combine to create an enjoyable television experience.

In the same manner, Christians have been given a system of divine laws and have no idea how to use them. You know, Jesus spent most of His time teaching His disciples and many others the basic operations and mechanics to Kingdom living. He would always teach in parables comparing the Kingdom in such ways as to a farmer and his field or a business contractor and his three mangers. Jesus was teaching Kingdom law. Jesus continually came up with sharp, vivid concepts that could further project and relay the operation of His Heavenly government.

People have become exasperated with Christian living because they have never been taught that they are living in a real Kingdom with a real King or how to operate His laws and principles to experience real change in their lives. Until the mentality that "God will do it all" changes in the hearts and minds of Christians, individuals will continue to experience minimal results in their Christian life, missing out on the greatest opportunity given to man.

The Kingdom of Heaven is God's entire blueprint for successful living and His perfect system for giving you the highest quality of life possible. You possess that system! It's been invested into you through the Holy Spirit, who ministers the reality of Heaven to your heart. We simply have to learn how to apply the correct force to God's supernatural laws in order to perpetuate an active manifestation of His government in our physical lives.

Let's look at another example through scripture that supports this principle of applying force. Jesus makes an interesting statement in Matthew 11:22. He says: *["Since the days of John the Baptist up until now, the kingdom has been <u>forcefully</u> advancing and "<u>forceful</u>" men lay hold of it."]* So to add to the question: Why do people fail to lay hold of the abundant Kingdom life? It's because they aren't taking an attitude of forcefulness! They aren't being forceful about the Blessing or taking an authoritative stand against fear-based living in order to see God's plan established in their life.

Let me put it this way: in order to lay hold of the Kingdom reality you have got to be aggressive, persistent and unrelenting about seeing the promises of God manifest. You have to get an attitude about what is rightfully yours. When you sense fear creeping in, or frustration and doubt trying to influence your words, you have to say "No, I'm blessed in the city and blessed in the field and I'm not speaking out of alignment with that Blessing!" You have to be like Jacob in the forest wrestling with God's angel (Genesis 32:26). He got fed up with the way things were, realized who he was in God and started putting a violent demand on it!

Are you fed up with the way things are yet? This is the attitude you've got to have. You have to let God know: "I know that I have the Blessing and I am not letting go until you start bringing it to pass in my life!" Everyday confront God with His Word, laws, principles, and promises. Declare in faith back to God what He said, and go about your day with an expectancy in your heart of seeing at least one of His promises fulfilled. This is applying force. Gradually you'll become more aware of and confident in the Word, and less timid about stepping out on it. You'll soon find that God loves nothing more than His own Word to be read back to Him so that He can fulfill whatever He's promised.

Aren't you tired of inconsistency in your faith walk? Do you want to really experience the abundance of Heaven's reality? Then get an attitude about possessing the Kingdom. Get forceful and start aggressively applying God's spiritual laws everyday so that you can begin to fully walk in the supernatural life that God always intended. As you do this, you can be sure that the limitations and boundaries of this cursed world life will began removing themselves from your reality spiritually, physically, emotionally, and financially! It's a guarantee that as you apply God's laws in everything you do, everything around you is going to change, immediately!

How Law Operates

It isn't your job to make any spiritual law perform its assignment, nor is it your job to make any particular thing you've prayed for come to pass. Law operates on its own and it does so the same way every time it has been activated.

Your position when it comes to Kingdom law is to:

1. Study it.
2. Gradually grow in its concepts.

3. Invest considerable time learning its function.
4. Apply accurate force to produce manifestation.

I want you to consider something: no one has to tell gravity how to do its job. Neither does anyone have to get up in the morning and give gravity a wake-up call saying "Hey don't forget to apply your force today and pull the mass of every object to itself." If gravity forgot or needed to be reminded how to do its job, we'd all be in big trouble. I think you get the point. You see, gravity is a natural law of nature; it was built into creation by God with its own purpose and function. Therefore it naturally performs its role in the earth as the force of gravitational pull. The only influence we have on gravity is the force we apply on it daily. This force comes from the constant mass that us humans, animals and other objects naturally place on it. As long as we exist in the earth, the laws of gravity will continue to function. If gravity had no mass to pull toward itself then it would have to become an inactive natural law. Law cannot cease to exist because it is unchanging, so that means it can only be active or inactive.

It's no different with Kingdom spiritual law. We shouldn't be worried about whether or not God's Word is going to come to pass. It's law, and the same principle applies in the spirit realm as it does in the earthly realm. What is seen (earth) has been made from what is unseen (spirit), so the concept of law didn't originate with science and human philosophy. It's a spiritual concept and it functions exactly the same under the same perimeters. The only difference with God's supernatural laws is there are no limitations to them. They exist in the spirit realm and are diametrically opposed to the laws of gravity, man-made religion, and any other limitations of natural laws that exist. God's laws exist from the beginning, superior to all cursed world laws and principles as well. Though "supernatural" laws exist outside of the earth, they have the manifested power to perform in the earth realm too. This is what you see happen when Jesus becomes human flesh (John 1:14); He is simply the manifestation of the Word or spiritual principles performing in the physical realm.

This takes the pressure out of faith, but leaves you and I responsible for applying force to see God's laws manifest their power. See, on the other side of Newton's 1st law of motion it states: "an object remains in uniform motion in a straight line unless a greater force is applied to change its state." What this means for you and I is once we've tapped into Kingdom law it is in continuous motion until a greater force stops it. Since God's supernatural laws are the highest invariable and functioning laws in Heaven and earth, when initiated in our lives they become constant and remain unchanging, radically shifting the lives of His people forever. This is why David writes: *"Your kingdom is an everlasting kingdom, and your dominion endures through all generations"* (Psalm 145:13).

Why? Well, there is no greater force in the universe, visible or invisible, that is strong enough to stop its perpetuation. When you establish a Kingdom law in your life, as long as you are consistent in it, it will always govern your reality, because there is nothing strong enough to stop it! This is so important, because as you begin to grasp the correct concept of operating in supernatural law and how it works, you become the architect of your life, building and designing the life you deserve through God's divine instrument. God wants you to realize that your job is not to "make" anything happen. Rather, it is to apply force to fully capable law and watch as it supersedes the normal regulations of this earth. Whatever spiritual law is sent out to do, it will accomplish every single time. This what God meant in Isaiah 55:11:

> *[A]s the heavens are higher than the earth, so are my ways higher than your ways and my thoughts than your thoughts. As the rain and the snow come down from heaven, and do not return to it without watering the earth and making it bud and flourish, so that*

it yields seed for the sower and bread for the eater, so is my word that goes out from my mouth: It will not return to me empty, but will accomplish what I desire and achieve the purpose for which I sent it.]

This is another misquoted and often misunderstood verse in the Bible. This scripture is not intended to prove to us how unreachable and ungraspable the mind of God is. Rather, it is simply God breaking down the science of Kingdom law plainly by using the laws of precipitation as an example. His "way" is His "way of doing things" as in His system or Kingdom, mentioned previously, operates solely by law. That Law encompasses His "thoughts" or "Word" which is the most intimate part of Him. That law is supernatural; that makes it supreme to any other law that exists, naturally or earthly. It makes sense then that God says His ways "are *higher* than the ways (laws) of earth."

God is only stating the principle that His system and its laws do not function according to the basic regiment of men and other worldly systems. He is saying: *"my law (way) is higher than yours!"* He is trying to teach us how spiritual law operates. So, as He is using the principles of precipitation, He is comparing the accuracy of His laws to the laws of snow and rain, and how they water the earth with an intended purpose to accomplish every time.

He is trying to express the same idea with His Kingdom law. Think about it like this: *if the laws of rain and snow know how to come down and complete an assignment, how much more does God's Word know how to go forth and accomplish what he's sent it to do?* So in other words, you never have to worry about anything you declare, believe or stand in faith for. God's law has the power to bring itself to pass. That literally means God's law possesses enough divine force, energy and authority to manifest itself. Now, lets take a closer look at John 1:14:

[The Word (law) became flesh and made His dwelling among us. We have seen His glory, the glory of the One and Only, who came from the father, full of grace and truth.]

"Became flesh" means to make manifest or take physical form. Now remember, Jesus is the "Head," the place from which the governing principles of God's Kingdom are formed. That's why He is the Word; He is God's perfect Law, supreme to all creation. Think about that, His Law is so powerful it literally took physical human form! You, as a part of His *body*, have complete access to that same spiritual law! You are apart of that supernatural law and it lives inside of you.

As a result, you can speak and declare the Word over anything, and by the nature of law it will perform its active duty. That's one of the key concepts to applying proper force to spiritual principle. We have to first acknowledge consistently on a daily basis that: 1) We are possessors of His law. 2) That His law works for us. 3) It has the ability to produce on its own.

Too often people get caught in the negative perception that they are responsible for how the Word performs or making it come to pass. This is bad philosophy. Also, it's thinking with a "fallen paradigm."

Remember in Eden, you aren't responsible for your provision, God is, and He does it through His pre-established law system. Don't become snared thinking you have to make His laws work; that's laborious and it's Babylonian. That would take the responsibility of your provision off of God and place it on you. You have overcome this state and paradigm through God's unlimited Blessing reawakened within you. If you get caught thinking you have to make it work, it will only cause confusion and greater frustration in your Kingdom pursuit. God doesn't want you to be confused about your part of the process when it comes to living according to His Word. Your job is to simply "send" the Word or apply accurate and consistent force to it until it begins to perpetuate itself into physical form. From there,

God's supernatural law is responsible for fulfilling itself. Whenever God's Word goes out from Him you can guarantee it isn't going to return until its assignment has been accomplished. Therefore, Kingdom living is not magic or a lucky rabbit's foot; as you can see it's plainly a matter of the simple science of applying spiritual law.

The Law of Wisdom

"Practice makes perfect." At least that's what most of us have been told growing up. The more you do something, naturally the better you become at it. That's the general idea when it comes to this statement. However, this statement is not always true. You could practice shooting or archery for a number of years but you'll never improve your accuracy if you're practicing the wrong way. What will happen is you will continue to get worse and worse and eventually you'll want to give up. In this sense practice would make *pitiful* rather than *perfect*.

The same idea applies to Christian living. Some individuals have been saved for a long time. They have been *"practicing"* Christians for over fifteen, twenty and thirty years. Yet, they struggle with getting prayers through, getting the sick healed or prospering in their personal lives.

Some Christians you meet are the most unpleasant people to be around. Why? They aren't pleased with the results they are getting in their own life. And though they have been "practicing and practicing" there is no sign of perfection or Heavenly influence because in the average Christian's life, they have been "practicing" *wrong*. So then, it would be inaccurate to state: when force is applied to Kingdom law it will always be perpetuated. A truer statement would be: when correct and accurate force is applied to Kingdom law it will always be perpetuated.

As I said, some people have been practicing or applying force for years but their understanding is bad; therefore their technique is bad and needs to be adjusted. You may be wondering if technique actually comes with using the Word of God. Yes, it really does. In fact the Word of God is more precious than anything on this planet. What makes us think that a level of skill is not needed to use it and actually get results?

If you look at any business, almost every field or profession requires some type of schooling, training or expertise in order for you to be considered employable in that area. It doesn't change with the Word of God. You have to learn it, and I don't mean one of those summer Bible challenges to see who can get through the entire book the fastest. It doesn't matter how many times you've been through the Bible if it's never been through you. As far as your "technique" goes, think of it of it as spiritual "archery" and that through correctly-guided practice God is trying to perfect your aim. Technique is determined by the "science" or systematic knowledge of something. When this knowledge is applied it is called skill: ability, coming from one's knowledge or practice, to do something well.

It doesn't matter how many times you've been through the Bible if it's never been through you.

> **It doesn't matter how many times you've been through the Bible if it's never been through you.**

God wants to produce spiritual skill in you through consistency in applying His Word until your life is perfected. He doesn't want to stop there though. God has given us His "gift" through the Spirit, who naturally teaches us how to understand God and His way of life. When skill (applied science) combines with a "gift" it's called "art." Through revelation of His Spirit and proper application of His divine laws, God's desire is to produce a work of art, a living manifestation of His reality for the world to see through the canvas of your life. This artistic expertise is called "Wisdom."

Ephesians 1:8 lets us know that everything we have accessed through Christ including spiritual (and material) Blessing, Heaven's abundance, forgiveness, and even redemption, is all predicated upon our ability to tap into wisdom. Wisdom is the ability to discern where something fits or where it goes. At the heart of wisdom you find the idea of craftsmanship or expertise as in a respective field or area of study. People who tap into God's wisdom are spiritual craftsmen who possess accuracy in applying the Word (Law).

Proverbs 4:7 says *"wisdom is the principal thing."* Wisdom is the most important element in the process of tapping into the Kingdom life. Without proper Word application in our lives, God's laws can have no effect on us. Just applying force isn't the answer, applying the "correct" force is essential. Companies spend millions of dollars every year to recruit and hire highly trained individuals who are skilled experts in their field. Why? Because they want trained people who know what they are doing working for them in hopes to produce the best possibility of increased sales and profits. The Kingdom is like this; it's God's spiritual machinery given to us along with a training manual and user guide called the "Bible" or His "Word".

If you'll notice when God was giving instructions to Israel on how to construct the High Priest's garment and all of its arrangements, He asked for *"skilled craftsmen and experts"* in their respective genres (Exodus 28:5, 15). What God was trying to show us is the wisdom it takes to skillfully operate the Kingdom and its laws. Ever since its birth the Church has had everything Christians have ever needed to create the life they want. The problem that exists is that they have not been taught how to properly use the manual. The Kingdom only works for people who are skilled at applying its principles. You must be relentless and constant about searching God's mind for strategic insight that can teach you to become skillful in applying His Word. Through patience, prayer and the leading of God's Spirit, you can use God's instruction to tap into the quality of Heaven's reality. Again, wisdom only responds when a genuine pursuit of its presence is sought out with a pure heart. Most people are too impatient, wanting God to do everything now. Wisdom will respond if you: 1) cry out to her, 2) learn her ways, and 3) allow her to show you how to apply the Word to experience supernatural success.

The Law of Understanding

Along with wisdom you must learn to tap into God's understanding. This is the ability to accurately grasp concepts and see into God's original idea and purpose for something. Understanding is the seed of wisdom producing a harvest of knowledge and applied skill for those who possess it. Thankfully as Christ's body, we are linked to all of God's original concepts (His head), which means that understanding is readily available for you to tap into. Without understanding, a law is simply dormant, meaning it is inactive rather that non-existent.

Remember that since law is invariable or constant, it is unchanging, meaning it cannot cease to exist. However, it can be inactive having no impact in your life. This is what the Apostle James meant when he said, *"Faith, if it is not accompanied by action, is dead"* (James 2:17). "Dead" here can literally mean to lie dormant, inactive or ceasing to have impact. Without understanding, a spiritual law can have no real influence in any sphere of your life. Kingdom law therefore is basically at rest until someone comes along and activates it through the force of faith, but only through wisdom and understanding. A great example of how this principle works is found in Matthew 8:26:

> *[Then he got into the boat and His disciples followed him. Suddenly a furious storm came up on the lake, so that the waves swept over the boat. But Jesus was sleeping. The disciples went and woke him,*

saying, "Lord, save us! We're going to drown!" He replied, "You of little faith, why are you so afraid?" Then he got up and rebuked the winds and the waves, and it was completely calm.]

Here Jesus represents Kingdom law. Notice, that Jesus is "resting," (lying dormant, inactive). Jesus is sleeping so hard during this storm, that the disciples became angry with Him and said "Hey, do you even care if we die out here?" Some accounts of this passage let us know that the storm was so bad that their boat was almost tipping over. Yet, Jesus was still asleep! This had to be a scary experience for the disciples. However, the type of fear they were operating in caused them to forget about who they were in the boat with. No matter how big the storms you face in life, don't allow fear to cause you to forget that Jesus is in the boat with you! Now, here Jesus is trying to teach them a valuable lesson on Kingdom law. After watching Jesus heal the sick and teach for hours on the Kingdom, it got late; however, Jesus wants to test what the disciples have learned. He wants them to grasp the concept of what's happening, and why every time He speaks the same results occur.

No matter how big the storms you face in life, don't allow fear to cause you to forget that Jesus is in the boat with you!

> No matter how big the storms you face in life, don't allow fear to cause you to forget that Jesus is in the boat with you!

You have to understand that everything Jesus ever did, whether healings, miracles, or signs and wonders, was simply a matter of Kingdom law operating in its nature. He always got the same results, no matter where He was. That's because law doesn't discriminate; it can't because it's invariable and unchanging. Therefore it doesn't know where it's functioning or who is tapping into it. It only takes into account the proper force that's being applied to it and immediately takes off to accomplish its work. This can only be done through understanding. Jesus, of course, doesn't want the disciples to be blind to what is happening; He wants them to have accurate knowledge in the science of His law so they can continually produce the same results as He did. He also desires the same for us.

Emotion doesn't move God, only law does.

So, Jesus intentionally sends the disciple into a storm, while He is sleeping. Again, imagine how

> Emotion doesn't move God, only law does.

frantic these guys must have been. To make matters worse Jesus is sleeping as if nothing is wrong! We know that in order for Jesus to sleep in that type of storm, He had to be in a deep rest. Meanwhile the disciples are kicking and screaming because they believe they are about to lose their lives. What's most interesting is no matter how hard they yell or how emotional they get, they cannot wake up Jesus (law). This is because emotion doesn't move God, only law does. Eventually to avoid the ship going under, Jesus gets up and calms the storm, but not before He rebukes their fear and teaches them a valuable lesson on the law of faith. He lets them know that neither fear or emotion are plausible ways to get anything from Him. God is a King, which means emotions don't move Him and He is only looking to see if you are in alignment with His divine law.

Supernatural law is the same way; it doesn't move because you yell, pray loud or pray for 10 hours. It is activated when proper understanding of faith is applied to it and then it will do exactly what it is sent to do. Until an understanding of how proper force is applied, just as Jesus was resting in the boat, Kingdom law will remain at rest toward us. Notice that after Jesus dealt with their fear, He turned around and finished the lesson by applying the law of faith immediately, speaking to the winds and the sea, and they both *"obeyed Him."* What happened? Jesus did exactly what He had been doing the whole time leading up to this situation: simply activating Kingdom law, applying accurate force through faith and then watching it accomplish its assignment.

You can't live outside of Kingdom law and expect to get the same results as Jesus with your life. As the body, we must always be aware of our "Head" by tapping into and allowing His concepts and principles to determine our circumstances. You may recall that every person that was healed by Jesus' ministry, He told them, "Your faith has made you whole." What did He mean? Since Jesus is the Kingdom and its perfect law, every time someone applied faith in Him, they activated the divine law of healing. However, Jesus lets them know that though He was the source, the manifestation of their healing wasn't coming from anything He did. It was coming from the law of faith and their ability to apply proper force on that law to accomplish exactly what they needed.

What does this mean for you? For one, you have to change the way you see God and how He operates altogether. How we see God in one area affects our entire life. The Gestalt Learning Theory presents a holistic approach to learning and proposes several laws of organization, which are innate ways that human beings organize perceptions. The core fundamental belief of this theory is that we as humans perceive situations as a whole, and that holistic perspective will essentially influence what actions we take. The Gestalt learning principles are much like the Hebrew concept of learning, which simply says: "if you don't do it then you haven't learned it." Our understanding of the Word trains our spiritual perception to see God correctly, how to apply His laws and how to live a supernatural life. Once we take on the correct perception of God as King, we will not separate Him from Jesus or His supernatural laws. Consequently, until we change our behavior, we haven't quite figured this out. However, that behavior is the result of a pattern of bad concepts and beliefs that we have toward Christian living.

If you don't do it then you haven't learned it.

We have to be intentional about adjusting those misaligned views through accurate understanding of God's truth and His purposes. We must be diligent about obtaining wisdom and understanding and filling our hearts with its revelation. Obey whatever God tells you to do. Before you know it, you'll be operating in the complete wisdom and knowledge of God becoming insightful and a possessor of great aptitude, quickly grasping Kingdom truth and applying it accurately to your life. This is how you create a reality shift: by gaining wisdom and understanding of God's Word. Again, everything we have been given in Christ is freely given, without any account of works. If something isn't working for us, it's not because God is keeping it from us, it's because we lack an accurate understanding of a Kingdom law and the proper wisdom of how to apply it. Thus every issue we face is a matter of inactive law we have failed to place force on. What that means is you really do have the power to change your world. The power to live above the limitations of life is in your hand and you are always one revelation away from creating that breakthrough you desire.

4

Supernatural Living II: Unleashing the Power of Faith

"For whatever is born of God overcomes the world; and this is the victory that has overcome the world—our faith." (John 5:4)

S o, what is Kingdom law? It is God's invariable and unchanging system of established principles set in order to supersede and govern all of the affairs of Heaven and earth. God is His law. Laws are simply keys by which we access all of the promises and abundance of Heaven. Law is created and intended to produce the same results every time it is applied. It is the predictable consequence of an action. Kingdom law is what I call "government policy." The Bible is full of God's policies and they never change because God, like His law, is constant. That means the results we are able to get with His supernatural laws are always the same once we've tapped into them.

Now again, although we have been given all that God has for us in Christ, we cannot access it or live in it until we learn how to function and operate in His laws. As I said earlier, when Jesus performed miracles, healings and great signs, He never jumped up and down and said "God, look what happened!" Why? Because in

Jesus' mind it was simply a matter of a higher law superseding an inferior one. He was functioning out of His "Head" (the governing laws and principles of Heaven's Kingdom) while He was in the earth. Therefore in Jesus' mind, no limitations existed, not one. I'm telling you that as a member of His righteous body, no limits should exist for you either.

In fact, that's one of the reasons God gave you His supernatural law; that you might experience life limit free, without boundaries and contrary to the voice of man and his carnal restrictions. Now, these "supernatural" laws of God are not the same laws commonly thought of as those mentioned in the Old and New Testament. It has nothing to do with works. It is a superior and spiritual law that governs the entire Heavenly and earthly realm.

Since what is seen has been made from what is unseen, this means the supernatural laws of God function at a higher authority and level than any of the earth's laws. It was out of these laws that we were created. In the mind of God where the abundant supply and resource of His supernatural creativity spring forth, exist all of His laws and governing principles of set order. This Law is Christ. We were created in that law, in its image, and joined to it in order that we too may live out of its unlimited authority and power. This supernatural law existed before time, and through it, the foundation and boundaries of earth were established.

When Adam fell, he gave up access to the paradigm that perceived the actual existence of these supreme laws, hindering his ability to think, act, and function beyond normal human capacities. So, where is God's "supernatural law" mentioned in the Bible?" In Romans 8:2:

> *[Therefore, there is now no condemnation for those who are in Christ Jesus, because through Christ Jesus the law of the Spirit of Life set me free from the law of sin and death.]*

The Bible is clear that another law, a spiritual one with far exceeding power than that of the earthly laws, exists. The higher of two spiritual laws is the *"law of the Spirit of life,"* or God's supernatural laws. It's in this law that we pre-existed and presently exist, unhindered and unbound by the limitations of satanic theory and doctrine. Remember, life is in the Blessing and death is from the curse. The Law of life is intended to represent the law of the Blessed world system and the law of death is intended to represent the law of the cursed world system. We, as heirs of Christ and members of God's royal family, are free from every trace of the cursed world system. Apostle James talks about the power concerning supernatural law as well in James 1:25:

> *[But the man who looks intently into the "perfect" law that gives freedom . . . . he will be blessed in what he does.]*

We, as heirs of Christ and members of God's royal family, are free from every trace of the cursed world system.

> We, as heirs of Christ and members of God's royal family, are free from every trace of the cursed world system.

We know that the Mosaic Law was not perfect or God would not have sent Christ. In fact, in Galatians 3:21 Paul reminds us that this previous law given had no power to give life. He says:

> *[For if a law had been given that could impart life, then righteousness would certainly have come by the law.]*

So then we know that until Christ came, there had been no spiritual power revealed to reclaim life in the Blessing. Now look again at what James says: *[But the man who looks intently into the "perfect" law that gives freedom . . . . he will be "Blessed" in what he does.]* That "perfect" law is God's highest law, pre-existing before all creation, possessing all the power and authority of Heaven. That Law gives us the Blessing and sets us free for good! Notice how James strategically links the perfect (spiritual) law with the Blessing, indicating that the impartation of that Blessing is dependent upon one's ability to look intently into (have understanding and wisdom of) that (perfect) supernatural law.

When Jesus told Peter He was giving him the keys to the Kingdom, He didn't fail to mention that whatever he "binds" on earth would be bound in Heaven and whatever he "loosed" on earth would be loosed in Heaven. What Jesus was simply saying was that He has given us access to all of the supernatural laws of the Kingdom, and depending which law we choose to place force on (bind) and what laws we make inactive (loose) we will see His Kingdom manifested.

The words "bind" and "loose" are government terminologies. Bind is the legal administrative power to create, establish, and enforce a legal ruling or law with all of its obligations. Loose is the legal administrative power to make law null and void or in active at the time, suspending its power and its obligations. These two terms have been commonly misunderstood in the church. Thus we have people trying to "bind" devils and "loose" them at the same time. If you understand the Greek use of these legal terms, then you'll know that grammatically it doesn't make sense to loose and bind in this manner. That scripture had nothing to do with spiritual warfare; that's why spiritual warfare wasn't mentioned there.

It was simply about the legal law enforcing power Christ was extending to His Church to enforce His supernatural regulations in earth. That spiritual law enforcement would then be responsible for producing the results of Heaven's manifested reality. By "binding" Kingdom law we are enforcing its unlimited regulations, and as a result we are "loosing," or making null and void and suspending, the limited laws of this earth realm.

Take a moment to think about this. God is telling you and I that what we allow in our life He has to allow. Why? Because God has given us not only free will but ruling authority to exercise that will however we choose. Since God is a King who operates by will and authority, He honors our authority and gives us the responsibility to produce the results we want to see in our lives. In essence, there is nothing negative in your life that you haven't allowed, whether it was through bad decisions, bad belief systems, or even speaking out of faith. Thankfully, God in His unlimited favor gives us grace, but that doesn't negate the reality that you are the gatekeeper and you must examine more closely: "*What have I let in lately?*" We as believers have to understand this, or we'll always be trapped with an imprisoned mentality of wondering why God did or didn't allow something. He gave you the keys, and the power to create the breakthrough you desire is standing right in front you.

Keys also imply doors. They give the idea of something we are trying to obtain as standing behind a door. Whatever is behind a door is unseen and therefore inaccessible. What this means then is that when Jesus gave us His spiritual laws (keys) He gave us access to what's behind the door, the ability to tangibly manifest what is unseen. God's promises of material blessing and monetary wealth are unseen. However, His supernatural keys empower you to make them a tangible reality.

Now, referring back to Romans 8:1-2, as far as those limitations of "*earthly or natural law,*" this is what Paul was referring to when he mentioned the "*law of sin and death.*" This includes all of the "cursed world system" with its earthly principles, philosophies, ideas, and perspectives. It is limited thinking. Its fallen paradigm just doesn't have the ability to rise above doubt and limitations. Remember that when Adam fell he lost his "righteous mind," or God's divine thought pattern. Much of our Kingdom pursuit is centered on reclaiming God's mind: the ability to think and expect above spiritual gravity. It is also the ability to perceive God's authority in us so that it can influence our physical reality. So the quality of life we experience depends upon which law we submit ourselves to. With this perspective in mind, look carefully at Romans 8:5:

[Those who live according to the [law of] the sinful nature have their minds set on that nature desires (natural law). Those who live according to the [law of] the Spirit have their minds set on what the Spirit (supernatural law) desires. The mind of the sinful man (one who functions out of earthly/natural laws and concepts) is death. But the mind controlled by the Spirit (supernatural law and all of its concepts) is life and peace.]

What this means is there are only two ways we as people can function in the earth: under God's supernatural laws or cursed world limited laws. By functioning out of God's laws we tap into His Blessing where the unlimited supply of Heaven exists. By functioning out of cursed world laws, we become confined and restrained from being able to live out our destinies as God-designed creatures made in the likeness of Christ. I am telling you that everything we will ever need for life, peace, prosperity, and abundance is one key away. We are one law away from tapping into God's endless supply and resources.

The Kingdom of Heaven is simply our ability to live out of the same unlimited thought capacity as our God.

We have to realize Heaven is God's "country" but He isn't confined to it. In the beginning existed only God and the infinite space of His creativity. Then from out of Himself, God produced the Heavens and earth. If in Christ (the Head), as His body, we pre-existed before these creations, then by being joined to Him we are automatically tapping into the unlimited riches we can access from His mind. The Kingdom of Heaven is simply our ability to live out of the same unlimited thought capacity as our God, who is Christ our Head, in the earth. When we learn to do this, we will no longer imagine any limitations because Christ has not imagined any either. As a result no limits will exist for you, only the ones you perceive are there. We should only be concerned with God's royal law, the law of Christ our King, the perfect law that gives freedom from every spiritual and mental limitation and boundary.

When we choose to live in fear and not trust God, we are leaning to the understanding of this world, applying force on its laws and warranting its manifestation in our life. That's why we have to be intentional about which laws we apply in our lives everyday.

Some of the ways we apply force to spiritual law is through:

- Our giving
- How we treat people
- The words we speak
- Where we invest our time

All these are concepts of applying force. If that force is under the wrong system, we only have ourselves to blame for not getting the results we desire to have. Those laws determine the system we are under, blessing or curse, thus determining our overall quality of life.

8 Simple Truths about God's Law:

1. It is "supernatural," making it the highest and most supreme law over all creation.
2. His law is invariable and unchanging, meaning it can never cease to exist. It is always available to you.
3. God's law can be inactive or dormant in your life if no force is applied to it.
4. Seeking God's wisdom and understanding is an essential element of releasing Kingdom law.
5. God does not discriminate who He blesses; it is simply a matter of tapping to His divine law.

6. God had already established you before creation, which means every law is legal for you to access and operate in.

7. Everything God has ever done was through law. He has already done all He is going to do and it is our responsibility to learn His law to receive His abundant life.

8. We are responsible for the results we get in life based on which law we submit ourselves to.

The Supreme Law of Faith

When faith is applied, results are inevitable. Our Bible is filled with account after account of the rewards of depending on God's Word. A successful life in God's Kingdom begins with a deep commitment to live by faith no matter what. Faith teaches and trains our hearts to concentrate on God's limitless ability and not our own abilities. This creates a disciplined heart that isn't swayed or tossed back and forth by the waves of life and an impenetrable faith impervious to the confines of this earth's systems. When anyone operates in the law of faith they rise above the limitations of their present surroundings to access the measureless power of Jesus.

As mentioned before, access to the Head means we have rights to function in all of God's laws. This also deals with the most supreme spiritual law, which is faith. Every law that exists in God's Kingdom is derived from faith and needs faith in order for it to work and function properly. Faith is the progenitor of supernatural law. Faith functions the same way every time. The law of faith is mentioned by Paul in Romans 3:27:

> *[Boasting is excluded on what grounds, on that of observing the law, no, rather on the law of faith.]*

If we want to get real results with faith in our lives, we have to understand that faith is law, and it has the power to bring anything to us. Also, being the most supreme law, we cannot forget that as we try to access other principles in the Kingdom we have to realize they cannot function without faith. For example, the law of sowing and reaping simply states: whatever a man sows, he reaps it. *Sowing* is an action, which means to accurately tap into this law you must be operating in faith. However most people fail to realize that *reaping* is just as much as an action as sowing, which means receiving your harvest will most likely require some step of faith to obtain too.

Most people fail to realize that reaping is just as much as an action as sowing, which means receiving your harvest will most likely require some step of faith to obtain too.

> Most people fail to realize that reaping is just as much as an action as sowing, which means receiving your harvest will most likely require some step of faith to obtain too.

Most people fail to realize this. They wait around for a harvest instead of reaping one. As a result they hardly see results with the seed faith principle. When operating in God's supernatural laws, an understanding of faith is always a necessity.

Through faith we tap into the richness of being a part of the "governing" body of Christ, which gives us superior ranking over every other system and authority in the earth. If we are the body joined to Christ and Christ is the first of all creation, then God had decided on the Church, the body, before the formation of the world. This means we precede all creation and we have total dominion over it.

Consequently man was not included in any of the limitations or boundaries God put on the earth. He made us outside of those boundaries and created us to exist within them, but never to be subject to them. It is because of the philosophies of religion and cursed world mindsets that Christians live beneath their power and inheritance.

Though they have the immense power of the Son within, they are subject to this world with limitation after limitation.

You still may find walking by faith a struggle, and it may seem as though once you that tap into faith, the gravity of earthly laws reminds you of your limits by telling you that you're too small, you don't have the credentials, you don't have enough money, etc. Regardless of the accusations you can overcome every earthly philosophy with a Kingdom truth. The key is deciding not to accept your present conditions as they are. You must continue to operate in the Word, taking giant steps of faith, and eventually faith will cut in and tell your situation, "I am superior!"

As mentioned before, the Wright brothers were told they could not build a flying aircraft because of the law of gravity. However, they didn't give up despite numerous failures and they discovered the law of lift. They didn't deny that the law of gravity existed; they simply tapped into a higher law. Imagine how they felt!

This should be the life of a true Kingdom citizen, lift! You are operating in spiritual lift every time you use your faith to contradict the normality around you. Just like the Wright brothers, you should never stop when you don't immediately get the results you desire. Keep looking and keep seeking the King, because there is always a law, a word, or divine instruction that can overcome your obstacle.

Keep looking and keep seeking the King, because there is always a law, a word, or divine instruction that can overcome your obstacle.

I want to encourage you that breaking into the law of faith is possible for anyone. Christ being our Head is our command center for Kingdom Law. He wants us to use His *head*, rather than ours. Actually when God tells you to live by faith He isn't asking you to use your faith; He is asking you to use His. Tapping into Jesus' head also means we have access to His faith! Our faith is still incomplete and developing since the fall of Adam. Christ, however, has prefect faith, and if we learn to live out of that realm of faith it will work for us every time.

What do you think happened to Peter when he was walking on the water to meet Jesus? Peter and the disciples were afraid but Peter was able to tap into Jesus' faith and imitate Him until he began to sink because of his fear, weakness, and limitations. It should also be noted that Peter grabbed Jesus' hand, indicating that he tapped back into Christ' faith (law). What people fail to realize is Jesus didn't carry Peter back to the boat; they walked back together on the water with Peter holding Jesus' hand.

That's you and I. We have to hold on to Jesus' hand, or tap into His faith law. God is saying to me and you "please use my faith, not yours!" God's faith is supreme and through His kingdom we have direct access to it.

The Law of Opportunity

It is also important for you to understand that God's richness does not consist of our world's currency system. God is a Spirit, so He has no need for our money. However, He can always show us where it is. We see an example of this when it comes time to pay annual taxes. (Matthew 14:27-28) Jesus gave Peter an instruction as to where the money was. Through Peter's obedience he would obtain enough money to cover not only Jesus' taxes, but the taxes for Peter's entire family. Of course the money was in a fish's mouth just as Jesus said. Now, the principle here is two-sided. First, Peter had a trade or skill, and through that trade, Jesus was able to bless him by instructing him on how to tap into Heaven's resource here on earth.

Notice that Jesus told Peter where the money was; He didn't give him any. It works this same way when we ask God for something. This brings me to my next point, the second principle in this passage.

Jesus at the most, is really a door opener. Now, I realize how that may sound, but as you pay close attention to the Bible and Jesus' life, you'll realize He was simply the door of opportunity for receiving. Again, Heaven can influence your reality as much as you want it to, but it's going to be through gifts and opportunity combined with your obedience. That's how you get what's in the spiritual kingdom into this physical earth realm. Jesus actually referred to Himself as a door opener in John 14:6:

[I am the "way," the truth and the life.]

The word "way" here literally expresses a doorway one walks through. What Jesus wants us to understand is that faith in Him is the door to which we access anything Heaven has supplied for us. Think about this, Jesus can't make someone do or receive anything; He is simply a way or opportunity to receive it. He is the "way" to salvation, eternal life, prosperity, and healing. His message always put the responsibility on the people to hear and believe His Word and take advantage of His Kingdom of opportunity. People who fail to realize this never truly grasp the art of living in the Kingdom.

For example, referring back to the "laws of sowing of reaping," many Christians have become frustrated with the seed faith principle or the law of sowing and reaping. Despite the controversy over this principle, it is mentioned all throughout the Bible, and is one of God's ways of guaranteeing that His promises show up in our physical life. One thing we need to be careful of is how we view these laws. Though we quote these principles together as one, they are actually two separate laws with their own separate functions. The accurate expression is the "law of sowing" and "the law of reaping." People will sow a financial seed but do absolutely nothing to "reap" their harvest. That makes no sense. Reaping is an action word, which means you will have to apply active faith to get your harvest.

Since faith is God's highest functioning law, every other law you tap into can only be activated through faith. What I found to be even more interesting is that one of the words for reap is "to realize." Yes, in order to reap your harvest you must realize the doors of opportunity God has place in front of you. Remember the Kingdom is a spiritual paradigm shift, which means its doors and authentic operation must be perceived also. Manifestation happens when your perception matches God's perception. That is the access point for materialization.

I am telling you, every time you name a seed and place it in the ground it is guaranteed to yield an immediate harvest. That's a Kingdom law; it never changes. The problem most Christians encounter is they are using a Kingdom law with no real understanding of how the Kingdom operates. As a result they expect their harvest to just fall in their lap. But the law of reaping doesn't teach that. There must be an act of faith applied to reap a harvest. Think about this: no farmer can stand in the middle of his field and reap a harvest.

If you pay closer attention to this principle of "open doors" you'll have results with the law of reaping every time. So what are you rich with? You're rich with endless and limitless doors of opportunity if you would become aware of them through a Kingdom paradigm or mindset. You must perceive those open doors correctly in order to manifest God's entire purpose and will as a tangible expression for others to see. Keep in mind there are no restrictions on how these doors can show up. You just have to be willing to walk through them once they've presented themselves.

You're rich with endless and limitless doors of opportunity if you would become aware of them through a Kingdom paradigm or mindset.

> You're rich with endless and limitless doors of opportunity if you would become aware of them through a Kingdom paradigm or mindset.

The moment you confess something, sow into the Kingdom or pray for healing, a door immediately opens up for you. If you are in expectation and paying attention, God will reveal to you what and where that door is. Just remember your response to what He provides is necessary for you to walk into your harvest. Regardless of how it looks, don't be afraid or procrastinate to walk through God's doors. How you feel is irrelevant, because you are living out of Christ's mind, not your emotion. Here Heaven's endless resources and supplies are waiting to overtake you.

By recognizing doors, you're tapping into the natural resources of the Kingdom where everything has already been "added" for you to enjoy out of the richness and abundance of Heaven's reality.

8 Truths Concerning the Supernatural Faith of God

1. Faith is God's most supreme law functioning in Heaven and earth.
2. Faith is the father of supernatural law, which means you cannot operate in any of God's laws without having tapped into faith. Without faith it's impossible to please (move) God.
3. The best way to break into this supernatural law of faith is to be willing to constantly take big steps of faith that are beyond your ability.
4. Confess, "I have the faith of God," every day.
5. Get out of emotions. When you function in the Spirit, the flesh has to die or become inactive to the supremacy of the anointing. You must learn to live out of your Spirit rather than your feelings.
6. God wants us to use His "Head," not ours. Adjust your approach to faith and begin pursuing God's faith not yours.
7. No matter what earthly system you face, God's supreme law of faith can overcome it.
8. Faith opens doors that must be walked through in order to reap our harvest.

The most important thing to always remember is that you don't control law. It operates on its own. No one has to tell gravity to work, because it is an established law with an assignment. I promise it's no different with faith. Once you tap into the law of faith, it's no longer you doing the work: faith is. Some people may feel like this is just "too easy!" No! It's the power of the Blessing. It makes rich and adds no sorrow to it (Proverbs 10:22). One of the things I always tell Christians is that faith, along with an application of God's laws, was intended to take the sweat out of living. Becoming dependent on Kingdom law can release you into a season of "rest" for the rest of your life!

5 More Truths about Kingdom Law

1. Kingdom law has the power to manifest itself.
2. Kingdom law was created to take the sweat out of life.
3. Applying the same Kingdom Law will always produce the same results.
4. Constant force on any law will cause it to be activated in your life.
5. Every Kingdom law is connected to faith. Without the law of faith working for you none of the other Kingdom laws will either.

5

Power Concepts I: Training and Engaging Your Thought Life

"We are what we think. All that we are arises with
our thoughts. With our thoughts, we make the
world."—Author Unknown

Change Concepts

The moment you believe something God has promised you, you have shaped a new idea or thought pattern. That idea has changed something in you and given you a renewed perspective to live out of. That new idea is called a concept. Concepts originate from your thoughts and the organization of those thoughts become ideas. The organization of those ideas result in concepts. Those concepts result in behaviors and life patterns we express through our everyday life.

If those concepts encourage a life beyond normal living conditions, they are flowing from the Blessing. However, if those thoughts and ideas lead you down a path of mundane living, their source flows from the spiritual gravity of the earth's cursed nature. But *"the Law of life (lift) has set your free from the patterns of death (gravity)."* You have to carry this truth in your heart wherever you go no matter the season of life. If you can replace the wrong concepts with healthy ones you can change the course of your future. By doing this you're not simply reshaping your thought life; you are reshaping your destiny.

The Power and Science of Thought Training

The concept of Christ living in you should not be taken lightly. This means there is someone else "at home" other than you. God's intent through His Kingdom is that as you submit your heart, will, and emotions to the King, you'll begin to live out of His ascended reality. The resurrected life of Jesus is that ascended place where He was raised and seated (in Heavenly places). He gives us direct access to that same empowerment.

The power of Christ living in us lies in His divine strategy to make His thoughts become ours. He wants us to take on His "Head". By taking on His Head, He means His thinking habits. This is so the realness of His lifestyle begins to create a total shift in ours. As Christ is our Head, we should be gradually transforming into His image, thought by thought, concept by concept. Paul made an interesting statement and presented the same revolutionary concept when he said: *"Let this same mind in Christ Jesus be in you also."* (Philippians 2:5). Can you imagine Jesus taking His mind, gift wrapping it and then presenting it to you saying: "Here is my mind; you can use all of its thoughts and strategies to live without limits just like I did?" That's what He did when He gave us His life. The only reason I could think of as to why someone would give you their mind is that they want you to have what's on it.

So, what's on your mind? Having Christ's thought energy affords us the availability of access to His entire thought wardrobe. Everything

He dresses His mind with He dresses ours with. This includes the creative power and ability to believe beyond all boundaries that whatever you can conceive you have the God-potential to achieve. The natural law and order of life can cause people to lose sight of His reality, causing them to lose hope of doing the seemingly impossible. Christ's thought power rejuvenates our minds and teaches and empowers us to believe and dream without limits again. Even when we find ourselves at times discouraged and entertaining thoughts of failure, Christ remains on the governing seat of our hearts, thinking about our victorious ending. He will always contradict those negative and defeated ideas with rich and life-generating pictures. His thoughts never change; they are to prosper you. They are filled with the spirit of expectation and overcoming power. Don't you feel like there's more you should be expecting out of a life designed by the Creator? If you're in a relationship with the King of the universe how should it impact the spiritual, physical, emotional, and financial areas of your life?

When you attempt to change concepts and adjust your outlook on life, you have to understand that you are not just changing perceptions; you are reshaping your identity. Your entire world is being altered with just one concept changed. This means your reality is shifting because you're tapping into your divine ability to create and build the life you desire. This is your chance to start over and make things new simply by renewing your mind and the concepts that you allow to govern it. Your thoughts are more than idol imaginations.

If you're in a relationship with the King of the universe how should it impact the spiritual, physical, emotional, and financial areas of your life?

If you're in a relationship with the King of the universe how should it impact the spiritual, physical, emotional, and financial areas of your life?

Thoughts are the result of thinking or mental activity. In other words, having thoughts is the by-product of having life. Our thoughts are the source of our being. They are the results of having an existence. Thoughts at their core are what a person experiences as a result of living while being a fully conscious, functioning human being. Thoughts are our main energy and life source. Thoughts tell us how to feel, how to perceive a thing, and how to determine what we need and want.

This also means then, that you are exchanging lives with Christ Jesus through the process of thought renewal. As you are adopting His thoughts you're being empowered by His richness and slowly transitioning into His complete and unhindered lifestyle. The power to change your life lies in your ability to change your thoughts by tapping into the blueprints of Christ and His spiritual DNA: His thought order.

You can train those new thought patterns and learn to live above the earth. You're not just imagining when you think on thoughts above. You are training your heart to actualize and encounter a new reality while creating a shift in how you perceive and view your walk of life. How do you see it now? How do you think some of those concepts, ideas, and perspective may be limiting you from receiving all that Christ has in store for you? Do you believe in a life without limitations? You have to be certain that a better life exists outside of the one you live and it was ordained for you to walk in. You can live in that reality.

Heaven is waiting on you to bring its atmosphere into the earth. Legally, that is the only way God's promises can function in His citizens' lives. Heaven is not just a place you encounter when you leave this life. Heaven is your home country and its government lives in you. When Jesus said, "The Kingdom is within you," He was impressing upon us a spiritual principle and foundational truth to all tangible Kingdom experience. That truth is that you can experience the tangible presence of Heaven now, and it starts with changing negative concepts that you have held onto that contradict everything that has to do with the Kingdom agenda. Your life is meant for healing, restoration, and complete living. Don't spend your time draining yourself with thoughts of failing. You can change anything you want if you believe it's possible. Your entire world will respond to what you are certain of and believe with all your heart. Your world is formed by behaviors that result from thought patterns. Quite simply put, you are what you think. Once again, Proverbs 23:7 makes it plain and clear: *"as a man thinks in his heart he is."*

You can change anything you want if you believe it's possible. Your entire world will respond to what you are certain of and believe with all your heart.

You must understand that although the mind is the power source of life, you should not be

> You can change anything you want if you believe it's possible. Your entire world will respond to what you are certain of and believe with all your heart.

subject to it. Your thoughts should be subject to what you say. Just as thoughts can influence words, words have the same ability to change a thought. What have you been feeding your mind lately? Depending on what concepts and ideas you submit your thoughts to, your quality of life will be determined. Out of the wellspring of those thoughts your identity, who you are and what you're really about will all spring forth through words, behaviors, and actions.

Just like an architect arranges and designs structures, you are establishing the foundation to your spiritual edifice with every idea you choose to think on. That "structure" becomes your living space and the place from which you live out of your physical reality. This was God's design from the beginning: that we, like Him, would become spiritual architects of our own lives by building our own thoughts and creating patterns of success that we desire to see based on His system of principles and spiritual laws. Do you believe this is possible? Can you see yourself as a spiritual master builder creating the life you've always wanted? God's plan is just that, to give you a life that functions out of His reality, impenetrable to the attacks of this modern day Babylon.

As we strive forward to live this *new life* in Christ, we are drawing from the substance of His ideas and the unlimited resource of His imagination. Now, how do we get His thoughts to change our thoughts so that we can experience His reality? Honesty is the first key. You have to be as straightforward with yourself as possible and you must be honest about what you've been believing.

This takes humility and patience to begin confronting those limited thoughts of doubt, fear, and unbelief. How do you feel about your life and what can you do to change some of those bad belief systems? What is your thought life like now? Write it down on a sheet of paper. Begin evaluating those thoughts and the inconsistency they may have with the promises of God. How do those thoughts fail to line up with the Word? From there, you have to rehearse the truth of God's promises until it becomes a part of your natural thought patterns, daily habits and confessions. You have to submerge yourself in Kingdom philosophy until it becomes your philosophy. That's what rehearsing God's promises does.

The Gestalt Learning Theory presents the idea that the mind is flexible and stretchable like a rubber band. It can grow, and it can shrink. The key to growth, as the Gestalt theory suggests, is pressure, but only under healthy conditions. When pressure is applied to the brain, it literally expands and retracts. The retracting is the reorganizing and fitting of the new data it has just received. The expanding is the process of learning or adding information. In order to create new space to retain the new information the brain increases its capacity. This is healthy pressure when you push your mind to receive new truth and add growth. When the brain retracts it stops short of its previous size as a result of the new information, leaving it larger than it was before.

On the other hand, when there is no pressure placed on the brain it stays the same size. This is the case with people who fail to take the time to feed their minds by reading books, studying God's Word, and challenging their normal thinking. In this case it would be exchanging erroneous thought patterns with ideas that exist, but are out of agreement with God's truth. Those are spiritual laws that we must get accustomed to in our belief systems to actually see them create change and have impact.

So, if you aren't learning, you're dying. In some cases the brain even shrinks for lack of pressure being added to it. You see, whatever you put in your mind will cause it to increase, decrease, or stay the same. Practicing the habit of thought training will empower your mind and stretch it with God's truth so that you can create space to receive Christ's mind. Let His thoughts shift you into another world. You were created to live in His mind. That was your divine being. In one sense, it's as though we have to learn to think the "right" way again by concentrating on the Word.

Repetition is the key to changing any thought pattern. Think about this example: How did you learn to ride a bike? You didn't read a 5 star manual on becoming the world's best bike rider. You learned by doing it over and over again because we, as humans, learn the best by repetition. That repetition creates persuasion: a strong confidence and belief in something. That's actually the heart of faith. When translated in Greek it means *"pistis"* or persuasion. What you are persuaded by determines what you live out. It's the idea of "immersion." You have to become deeply absorbed by something by your continuous practice of it.

God wants you to become immersed in the Word through daily repetition in it. By doing this you are practicing His thoughts. Rehearse them out loud as well. Soon those contradictory thoughts will leave and the ideas of Christ will begin to govern your heart and then your physical reality. Training our mind is like riding a bike. We learn by getting on, falling off, and repeating that same process until we become convinced and educated on how to live out that new Kingdom truth. By doing this repetition you are training your heart and thought habits to believe only what the Word says. If you train your ear to what God promises they become the center of your thoughts.

The greatest thing about learning to ride a bike is that you never forget how. In the same way, as we catch onto this process of cultivating a healthy thought life we are creating a skill that will last us a lifetime. As you change your concepts, areas of your life that didn't reflect the promises and paths of God will begin to line up and flow in that same direction.

Even as you make the adjustments mentally you'll have to guard those new ideas. That's another reason we must train in the Word. As you speak the Word daily, faith is being released and becomes a light to dark thoughts. It acts as a thought repellant to any negative mindset trying to creep back into the spiritual homes we've built.

Every chaotic and out of order area in your life begins with a stronghold in your mind.

> **Every chaotic and out of order area in your life begins with a stronghold in your mind.**

We have no reason to ever accept defeat. Nowhere in God's blueprint does an outline for losing exist. Every strategy God has divinely invested into us through His Word is a plan to overcome. This means when we experience doubt and fear of any kind it doesn't come from the faith that was deposited into our hearts through God's mind and Spirit. Every chaotic and out of order area in your life begins with a stronghold in your mind. That's where the real battle is taking place. We have to use the spiritual repellant of faith by taking authority over every idea that riots against God's favor towards us. This is our supernatural power mentioned in 2 Corinthians 10:4-5:

> *[The weapons we fight with are not the weapons of the world. On the contrary, they have divine power to demolish strongholds. We break down every thought and imagination that sets itself up against the knowledge of God, and we take captive every thought to make it obedient to Christ.]*

Let your thoughts take you to a whole new level of living. When the gravity of negative ideas tries to pull you down, be resistant by declaring faith, and watch those negative forces flee from you. God wants you to know that you are free to dream without limits, full of creative imagination, because it is your Father's good pleasure to give you His Kingdom; the place of His abundant supply.

Take every thought that doesn't line up with God's plan captive and obedient to the unfailing love found in God's Word. You are blessed, you are favored, you are graced to succeed, and you are destined with the sovereign plan of royalty. Now say so!

As you are continually drawing from the richness of God's thought supply, you are tapping into His supernatural life.

Framing Your World with Words

As you retrain your thinking habits, those thoughts and ideas naturally transform into Word power that you speak and declare over your life. Jesus said, *"Out of the abundance of the heart the mouth speaks"* (Matthew 12:34). Your positive confession should naturally emerge from the positive conversation you're having within yourself.

As you retrain your thinking habits, those thoughts and ideas naturally transform into Word power that you speak and declare over your life. Your positive confession should naturally emerge from the positive conversation you're having within yourself.

> As you retrain your thinking habits, those thoughts and ideas naturally transform into Word power that you speak and declare over your life. Your positive confession should naturally emerge from the positive conversation you're having within yourself.

Those words have the power to frame your physical life, so as long as keep saying those same things, nothing will be able to change what you've established. Remember the same words God spoke that set the sun in place have been holding that sun in place even up to this very day. The same life-forming power is in you. Let your words flow from the healthy and positive perspective you are gaining from the Word. As it transforms your vocabulary it will transform your life. Simply put, words are the tangible energy of thoughts that can frame our worlds.

Power Results

I remember a time in my life when I was on the verge of losing my vehicle. I was drastically behind in payments and didn't know what to do. It was my 2nd year in full time ministry and things were not going the way I had imagined them. I remember getting a call from the company I was leasing from letting me know they were going to take my car that day. I became discouraged as the calls kept coming in, one after another to remind me I was about to lose my only vehicle.

As the emotions of shame and embarrassment grew strong, I felt the gravity of fear and doubt beginning to pull against my hope. Suddenly in the midst of that chaos, I heard God gently whisper a scripture in my heart. He said, "Anything is possible to him who believes." I had always thought I knew what that scripture meant, but God was about to transform my understanding of it. As I began to think and meditate on that spiritual truth (law), another scripture came to mind. I recalled that Jesus once told His disciples that all power was in His hands and that He was giving it to them. This caused me to realize that even though I couldn't see the money in my account physically, there was still something I could do to determine my outcome. Some kind of power was in my hand, but it was up to me to figure out what that power was.

As I thought about it more, it became clear to me that through those scriptures God was stirring my heart. He was actually inspiring an expectation and drive in me to recognize the faith I already had and to not give up. More negative phone calls began to come in, and still I continued to meditate on those principles and speak favorably over my situation. The more I meditated on the Word, the quieter the voices on the phone got and the louder the voice of God became.

His truth and His reality became my concentration, not what anyone else was saying. I sensed the Word beginning to perpetuate itself within my spirit and suddenly I realized that creating the faith I needed was not my responsibility; it was spiritual law already there, waiting for me to tap into it. I also came to understand that it was not my responsibility to make what I had been believing for come to pass. Again that job belonged to God and His divine law.

Thankfully I soon felt the weight of discouragement lift even though my financial situation hadn't physically changed yet. But, it didn't matter to me what I could see with my eyes, because the pressure was not on me anymore. I had transferred it to the power of God's supernatural law. I discovered that my only responsibility was thinking rightly about the Word and my situation, perceiving it correctly through God's perception and steadily applying force on faith through how I was thinking and speaking. This was allowing God to do His job! After becoming so immersed in those principles I was empowered to do something I had never done before.

I went outside and laid my hands on the car and declared and decreed that it was no longer mine and was now under the possession of Heaven, thus making it official government property of the Kingdom. (By the way, I actually said all of that. I may have over done it a little bit, but I wanted to make sure I was speaking the right things!) I determined that since the car did not belong to the system of the earth any longer, man couldn't take it from me.

Amazingly, the day went by and the car was still there. A week went by and my car remained in the driveway. Another week went by and still the same result: my vehicle had not been taken from me. Five months went by and they had not taken my car! What happened? Well, for one, I adjusted my thoughts and concentration toward the power of God's Word to fulfill itself and not on my limited ability to come up with the money. Secondly, I had continued to speak positively with the Word over my situation despite my emotions and feelings! Thirdly, I had realized by then my faith and confession generated enough power to create new opportunity for a positive outcome.

Naturally I was propelled into action by activating my faith. Even though one law had been spoken by the leasing company, which was, *"You're going to lose your car,"* I had released a higher law that said: *"You cannot take my car."* This gave Heaven the opportunity to begin to reshape and reform my reality based on its pre-designed outcome for me rather than what man had decided. Not only that, I was now aware that by submitting my situation to the unlimited power of the Kingdom, I had removed all limitations from God's ability to work things out in my favor. I'm telling you, I was excited, because I had no idea that these things could actually work for me until God exposed to me the reality of His government.

The best part of the story is that once I saw my previous confession work, I implemented a new statement of faith. I knew that if it worked once, it had to work again, because law is invariable. It's unchanging. I began to declare that my remaining debt of car payments would be cancelled! Can you believe that?

Well, sure enough after a couple more months the leasing company eventually contacted me to let me know they were going to cancel the past due payments and allow me to turn in my vehicle and complete my leasing contract free and clear! The key was I changed concepts about the car, who it belonged to, and who's reality I was going to submit myself to. In my mind it became God's car and no longer mine, and His Word had the last governing authority over whether or not I kept it.

What happened with my car is a matter of the operation of law. That's the way things work in the Kingdom and that should be the result every time the Word of God is used. It's no different than the time Jesus fed the 5,000 people (John 6:1-15) with a small amount of fish and loaves of bread. He was simply operating under the same spiritual principle. Jesus knew there wasn't enough food to feed every person, yet He asked the disciples to bring Him what food they did have.

Right here, Jesus was saying to them (and also telling you and me): "There is always something in your hand that can change your situation." Jesus knew that if He could get His hands on what little they did have it would become subject to the authority of the Blessing, meaning that Heaven's reality would become the governing factor and source, no longer the laws of man. Of course it worked. Not once but Jesus did the same miracle again not long after! (Mark 8:1-10). Again, that's because supernatural law always works once you have tapped into it and as long as the same continuous force is applied, nothing can stop that law from its perpetual activity. It will continue to create favorable conditions for you!

Now, take notice that Jesus "blessed" the bread and the fish. Why did He do that? Because the Blessing was all the power needed to reactivate the assignment previously placed on the fish kingdom in the book of Genesis 1:22 which was to *"be fruitful, increase in number and multiply."* Think about that, when Jesus spoke the Blessing over that fish it changed systems and immediately became subject to the original authority and order in which it had been established in the Garden of Eden. As a result it began to function under the same spiritual law, even though it was dead!

That's the power of the Blessing and what happens every time we allow the Word to govern our situation. The original plan and intent of God is manifested, making everything subject to His abundant grace prepared for us since the beginning of time. If you are committed to living in the Blessing and speaking words of blessing, everything has to come into alignment with God's original plan intended for it.

One last point I'd like to reiterate about the experience with my car is that I stopped calling that car mine and I started saying it belonged to God. I heard Dr. Myles Munroe say once, "As long as we call something ours only, that makes us solely responsible for it." However, when we say that it belongs to God, the automatic provision and abundant supply of Heaven must make provision and cover all of our possessions. If you want to see Heaven influence your life, you have to change how you see it and what you say about your situation and your possession. Start calling it God's so that He will become responsible for it, and not you. I found that often times it's really that simple: many of the issues that Christians are facing today are simply a matter of them needing to bring things to the Lord and submitting them under His rule.

Now, let me take a moment to point out that there are a lot of people who hear this type of message and began thinking, "Yeah right." Some people may hear about the testimony concerning my car and think there's something weird going on. However, if you don't believe this could ever happen, that settles it all right there, because it will never work for you. If Jesus was here and He got those types of results most Christians would praise God! Why should you accept anything less than the same for your life? The fact of the matter is that this was not a matter of logic or reasoning; it was a matter of God's word, which is higher law overriding the law of man. People will always have a different report, but it is up to us to choose which report we will believe.

You have to decide which reality you are going subject your mind to: the limited wisdom of man or God's infinite creative ability! Who do you believe? What do you say it is? I hear people often say "It is what it is." But, by making confessions like that you're giving permission for things to stay the same.

That type of thinking just leaves your circumstance up for grabs to anyone or anything. It is what YOU say it is and you have to determine that there are no boundaries to what can happen when you depend on the Word of God! I want to make it clear that this way of living isn't an illusive concept or "pie in the sky theory." And it certainly isn't a way to escape the responsibilities one has in life. This type of living makes you responsible for what happens in your life based on what you allow through words, philosophy, and the actions you take to see things come to pass.

It is what YOU say it is and you have to determine that there are no boundaries to what can happen when you depend on the Word of God!

> **It is what YOU say it is and you have to determine that there are no boundaries to what can happen when you depend on the Word of God!**

It's called results-oriented living and it's designed for you to get real results with the Kingdom, free from the limits of average mundane living. God has set you free! Be free to release your faith and expect Him to do the unimaginable. He's waiting for you to put your faith in a place your mind has never gone so that He can get something over to you today that you didn't have access to yesterday.

The Concept of a Winning Solution

Again, the entire purpose for Jesus recovering the Kingdom was to give the authority and power over life back to us! Simply put, He wanted to make you responsible for the results you get out of your life. Look at Matthew 28:18-19:

> *[Jesus approached and, breaking the silence, said to them, "All authority (all power of rule) in heaven and on earth has been given to me. Go then and make disciples of all the nations, baptizing*

them into the name of the Father and of the Son and of the Holy Spirit."]

Notice that the first thing Jesus does after He has recovered total power and authority of the Kingdom, He puts that same power and authority right back into the hands of His people and instructs them to now duplicate the very things they've seen Him do in their lives! Breakthrough really begins at the moment we truly decide we have all the power we need in Christ for successful living. We have to discipline ourselves to this truth: that we are the only ones responsible for the results we get out of our lives and no one else. By this, I mean the actions we decide to consciously take everyday according to the Word to see God's truth governing every sphere of our reality.

I become concerned when I hear people use negative experiences of their past as reasons for not achieving the success that they desire. You may have experienced hurt in a bad relationship, been neglected as a child, or got involved with the wrong crowds at some point in your life. We all have made some poor choices. Regardless of the situation, we have to truly understand that it is ultimately the decisions that we make that determine our destinies. To place blame on someone, or something that's been done to you is to take the power that you have in your own life and transfer it to something else. The moment you accept the idea that someone else may be responsible for unfavorable conditions in your life you've disempowered yourself.

Many Christians have become deceived with the concept of Satan and have used him as an excuse to not pursue or obtain everything God has commanded us to.

Many Christians have become deceived with the concept of Satan and have used him as an excuse to not pursue or obtain everything God has commanded us to.

One of the saddest things to see is Christians who believe the devil is responsible for all of the negativity in their lives. Many Christians have become deceived with the concept of Satan and have used him as an excuse to not pursue or obtain everything God has commanded us to. When Jesus first presented the idea of an adversary, He was very quick to let His disciples know that most of what they thought they knew about him was probably untrue. John 8:44:

[For he is a liar and is the father of lies.]

I understand the way that scripture is usually read and interpreted, but let me help you understand what Jesus really meant. Jesus calls him a liar as if to indicate the irrelevancy of his existence in the believer's life! Jesus also calls the devil a father and those who believe his lies are his children. We have to understand that when the devil lies to us, he speaks through people in the earth.

What this statement also means is in relation to the liberation and unlimited dominion a person accesses through the Blessing when they receive God's favor and increase. The moment we become inhabitants of Christ's government, we receive all of the benefits of the completed work of the cross. One of those benefits is total liberation from the impact of the darkness in our lives as mentioned in Colossians 2:14-15:

[Having canceled the charge of our legal indebtedness, which stood against us and condemned us; he has taken it away, nailing it to the cross. And having disarmed the powers and authorities, he made a public spectacle of them, triumphing over them by the cross.]

The term 'disarm' here literally means to demilitarize an entire military camp by seizing all of their weapons. This is why we are warned by the writer in Colossians 2:8 to be sure that we are not held captive by *deceptive philosophies or 'bad thinking'*. Where our lives meet the finished work of the cross, the potential impact of darkness and satanic influence is totally eradicated from us. It's imperative that every Christian understands and values this.

Though this may contradict a lot of common reasoning in the church, we need to know that in this verse God is plainly telling us that He eliminated the ability of Satan to harm us. The only enablement the enemy has to influence our lives is contingent upon the belief systems and actions of believers. Jesus' cross put the satanic kingdom and all of its laws under our feet, in other words you are in a superior Kingdom, therefore you have superior rank over every force that would come against you! You're enemy has been disarmed it is your responsibility to walk in this understanding and confidence.

Since we have been raised and seated with Him (Ephesians 2:6) in the Heavenly Kingdom, by the law of faith we have become sons of God, making us beneficiaries of the contract God made with the father of faith, Abraham.

Again, that same Blessing is on you and the power of that Blessing restores to you the same ability given to Adam in the Garden of Eden. God blessed him and told him to take full authority and power over his environment. Though things around us may not seem this way, there are rivers of Eden flowing within you and your responsibility is to influence a dying world with the love, compassion, peace, and prosperity of Eden's Garden within your soul.

So remember, you've already overcome your greatest mountain. If you can keep your eyes fixed on the victory God's already given you through His Son, you won't allow anyone to determine what you get out of your life besides yourself. The responsibility is on you to possess the life you want. Go and possess it!

Remember that when God tells us to take dominion, His expectation of our complete success is based on the power and favor He has empowered us with through His Kingdom! This is why it is important that people do not become self-bound by entertaining the idea that anyone can somehow stop the purpose of God in their life.

The moment you believe that, you empower it to happen. The power is in you. It's in your hand and you can change things now.

The Power of Healing Thoughts

So what am I saying to you? That you've already won, and the Blessing is that winning solution. It's the concept that God has already given us victory over our enemy so we don't need to exhaust ourselves with religious teaching that makes us worried about the devil. The real battle you face is not with people or through the physical perimeters of this life. It's getting your heart to line up with the truth of God's Word that He has already healed you and made you safe from the attacks of your enemies. It's a struggle that's fought in the battlefield of the mind because our thoughts are the unseen place from which the source of life truly flows. Proverbs 4:23 puts it this way:

> *[Keep your heart with all vigilance, for from it flows the springs of life.]*

So you see, the real problems we face flow from within us, our thoughts, and our imaginations; the gateways of our souls. Your best weapons against these battles are using the force of expectation, applying God's truth, fixing your thoughts on Heavenly things, and speaking favorably over every situation no matter what it is. The key to a prosperous life begins with the soul. God wants to make sure you understand that your quality of life is dependent upon your ability to manage your thoughts, emotions, and words. Don't let past failures or defeats keep you from getting up again. Don't allow a divorce, or broken relationship to cause you to fear loving again. These are internal wounds that paralyze your forward motion in life by causing you to major on your past.

You can positively influence your overall life by taking control of your thoughts with the healing promises God has made in His Word. The first step begins with claiming those promises and saying that you're healed even though you may not feel it at first. Remember faith is not emotional; it's law, so feelings have nothing to do with it. Keep saying and believing that Jesus healed those scars of the past, with His stripes and the blood shed on His cross. He bore your pain, your grief and guilt of past shameful ways. In yourself you have to know you are free.

Let the Word of God set you free by meditating on its truths. You can be completely sure that Jesus will begin to minister to those wounds and cause the burden and weight of your past to gradually melt away. Don't let discouraging thoughts come in and live there! Kick them out. Give every toxic thought this notice: *"It's time for you to go, because I cannot allow you to spoil the good God wants to do in my life."* Speak to yourself while standing in the mirror if you have to and say what God says about you. Keep looking at God's Word, not your inadequacies or the insecurities you have. You have everything you need through Christ to begin experiencing your new life, the life you are truly meant to lead, the life you've always deserved!

A Healthy Philosophy

As I mentioned earlier in Colossians 2, the writer warns us not to become bound or "held captive" by taking in *"hollow and deceptive philosophy,"* making the results we get in our life a direct reflection of what we think! See, every chaotic area in our lives exists as a result of bad information we have taken in and a lack of Kingdom truth being applied in that particular area. If there are traces of negativity continually showing up in certain areas of your life, it's because somewhere along the way you believed a lie. Your philosophy about something needs to change.

For some people they can't seem to get out of doubt or break the cycle of poverty in their life. This usually begins with a principle or commonly held belief that was instilled in them growing up. Some of the environments individuals were raised in don't encourage economic empowerment. A mentality of bad money management is at the heart of many challenged communities, and until people change their attitudes about what money is, how it is used, and what God wants to do with it, the same cycle of debt will continue.

Another example is when individuals struggle finding their soul mate. Oftentimes people will say things such as "I just can't find the right person" or "there are no good women/men in this city." As a result they become subject to what they have spoken, as their words are just a release of the negative energy they have been holding onto through bad philosophy. A good example of this occurred in one of my Life Enrichment Seminars while I was in Omaha, Nebraska. During the seminar God placed it on my heart to address a negative mentality that some women have when it comes to finding a good, faith-filled, Christian man. See, if you aren't careful, your failures in past relationships can become hindrances to what you're able to believe and receive what God wants to give you now.

In this particular session, I challenged the women to confront some of those negative mentalities toward finding a good man. We began to pray and break some of the word contracts that they had made through bad philosophies and negative thinking toward men. They were surprised to learn about the limitations they were placing on God to perform His Word in their lives because of the agreement they had with those negative philosophies. I simply helped them to confront those negative mindsets, broke them off with the Word, and implanted new and healthy philosophies by agreeing with God that He did have good men waiting for them and that He was well and able to draw them.

Within weeks, testimonies began to come in from all over. In fact the church we held it in experienced several engagements/marriages as a result. Women that attended the seminar found themselves being approached by well-qualified, single Christian men. What happened was a change in the philosophy was like breaking a negative contract allowing the Word of God to fulfill its assignment.

Until you get the right Kingdom truth and apply it, the same cycle will continue no matter how much you pray, cry, or even yell. Remember that since God is a spiritual King, emotions do not move Him, only His law does. In other words, you should be asking God for insight and strategy. Don't look for God to just do it for you once and right now, but ask Him for strategies that will last you a lifetime. God wants to teach you how to fish so that you can have food for life. This is called praying for Kingdom strategies or divine implementation.

One of those strategies is to strategically attack toxic philosophies, exchanging them with what the Word says and developing that concept as a new thought pattern and way of thinking. Maybe there are some bad philosophies you've held onto about certain things in your life. God wants to bring change to those places and cause new rivers to flow in the dry areas of your life.

What are some negative ideas about yourself, your life, and your financial situation that you need to change? You should write them down and find scriptural truth that contradicts those thoughts and ideas. Changing those negative outlooks will change the results you are getting in that area of your life. Don't stop in one area as you begin to see results, apply this strategy to every area of your life. Divine implantation is a life key to living above limitations.

How Purpose Gives Provision

You see, in Genesis, every place that didn't reflect God's glory existed as a result of the Blessing not being enforced in that area. This was one of God's purposes for creating man, to take His Kingdom and divinely influence every chaotic area in the earth with His nature.

The more we understand this, the more we can live in our purpose, which empowers us to walk triumphantly through every season of life.

Purpose *is* power! Wherein lies God's original intention, you will find the power to fulfill that intent also. In other words, most believers do not walk in the fullness of the measure of Christ's power because they don't have a mature revelation of their royal position in heaven or their purpose for existing there. Oftentimes people try to pursue a purpose that wasn't ordained by their Creator. When this happens they become frustrated because God has not made provision outside of His original idea and plan.

Even though the Word clearly tells us that God gives us power through His Spirit, most people rarely experience this blessing because they are outside of God's original purpose for their life. You cannot decide your purpose, because you didn't create yourself. You can only discover it. When you function outside of that original purpose you lack the power for victorious living because there is no provision made for you outside of God's purpose for your life.

Functioning within God's original intent allows you to understand your true identity as a son of God. Since provision flows from the same place of God's purpose, His heart, this automatically gives you access to the power and tools needed to function in and fulfill that purpose. You never have to worry when you know you are functioning in God's divine assignment for your life. One way to escape fear rests in the confidence that flows from a sure heart that knows it's operating in the complete purpose and destiny of God.

My Promise, My Faith, My Responsibility

Every day I fill myself with the promises of God's Word and remind myself that I have a divine blood-right to God's benefits that exist as a result of my connection with Jesus. This helps me to remember that no one has the right to produce any results in my life that I don't desire. Most people think that Jesus came to take power and keep it, but again, the first thing Jesus did when He received all power in heaven and earth was turn to His disciples and say "now, I give it to you". This is because Jesus came to put the power of victorious living back into the hands of the people. Throughout Jesus' healing ministry, He was quick to let individuals know that the responsibility for their healing, deliverance, and breakthrough was on them. To function opposite of that truth contradicts God's purpose for creating man in His likeness with His abilities and creative imagination. Notice throughout the Bible, Jesus is consistent in reminding individuals after they have received a miracle from Him that *their* faith was what made *them* whole. As long as you understand the potential of breakthrough that rests in you and your passion to see it released, you'll always be standing in the place of favor and in perfect position to accelerate to the next season of blessings.

Spirit-Led Kingdom Training

This idea that the responsibility for breakthrough is on the believer is a foreign concept to many Christians, but it's pure biblical-based truth. To go further, I'm going to tell you that God Himself isn't responsible for the results you get in your life, you are! In fact, to show you how true this is, God will allow us, at times, to make poor choices just so that we understand how responsible for our own lives we really are.

One thing that has held most people back from salvation is the negative perspective that most religious institutions have painted through religious rhetoric, dogma, and practices. They see people who place all kinds of rules on others' lives and dictate what it is that they can and cannot do. As a result they believe that this is what God is like and that's what He wants to do with their life. It is actually the contrary! God's desire is for you to take control of your life and get the best results possible by using His principles. Whether or not you use them is up to you. You see, God gets the most glory out of your life when it works on its own, just like His spiritual laws.

As a manager in sales years ago, I found that my job was much easier and enjoyable when I didn't have to micro-manage, and my employees could effectively do their jobs without asking me how to do everything. It also made me look better as a teacher and coach. God gives us His Holy Spirit as a personal trainer to teach us His system to perfection so that we can take control of our lives using His principles.

So take advantage, and daily seek the Holy Spirit for His success principles. The same divine principles He gave the patriarchs of the Bible He will give to you if you are persistent in asking. It's our responsibility to hunger after God's Kingdom and its spiritual principles by constantly sitting at the feet of the Holy Spirit. He wants to teach us how the Kingdom works and how to effectively apply its power. His assignment is to teach us how to build and create the lives we desire so that every area of our life resembles the Kingdom. In a Kingdom it's important that the lives of the citizens glorify the King and His nature.

Think about it like this: once a parent has raised a child, their greatest joy comes not when the child has to continue to come to them for everything, but when the fruit of their parental guidance begins to take manifestation through great decision making of their child. God is the same; He gives us tools, creative learning, and a personal performance trainer to teach us how to live victoriously. At some point we all must move on into spiritual maturity in order to be the conquerors He has called and predestined us to be. This involves making a commitment to take responsibility for our own lives and remain conscious of the unlimited possibilities that exist through our faith in Him.

At some point we all must move on into spiritual maturity in order to be the conquerors He has called and predestined us to be.

We also have to be committed to not making excuses for failure and placing the power of our own life into someone else's hand. Every

> At some point we all must move on into spiritual maturity in order to be the conquerors He has called and predestined us to be.

person should recognize the treasure and gift of life. Its value is immeasurable despite the difficulties we may face while here. This should be motivation to cherish life, take possession of it, and live it to the fullest. You can rise above any limitation. Don't let anyone or anything hold you down or believe that someone else is responsible for your breakthrough.

That is spiritual gravity and that philosophy will only cause you to remain limited to what people think. For this reason, you should realize there is no time for self-pity, regret, or blame. I determined a long time ago that I'm not transferring any power over my life to someone else. You should do the same. Value your life enough to take control of it and become responsible for your future and its success.

For so long people have been afraid to use the word "control" in the church as though it somehow negates the existence of God's power or usefulness in our lives. Some feel that everything is in God's control and He will handle it all. If that was true, then you have to ask yourself, why are there so many areas of your life you aren't pleased with? Is God in control of that? Are the negative reoccurring cycles orchestrated by God as some divine strategy to show you how much He is in control by making your life difficult? People who think like this never take control of their destiny and die wishing they had done so much more than what they accomplished.

God is not discredited when we take control; He is glorified. He created us in His image to reflect His behaviors and life patterns. God gets results. He wants the same for you and I, and His Kingdom is the module to ensure that happens. Don't unwisely invest your time waiting for life to happen, because all that will happen is it will pass you by. Control isn't a bad word; it's a Kingdom Word and it's another word for dominion. This concept is healthy to adopt as long as you balance it with the understanding that some circumstances we encounter are unforeseeable and out of our determining.

The truth is sometimes we cannot escape the realities of this fallen and broken world. It helps as a reminder that we still have something better to look forward to after this life. This means understanding our jurisdiction when it comes to the Kingdom, which comes with every law, in order to correctly use our power and authority.

With this in mind, one should never waste energy worrying about situations they have no control over or are out of their jurisdiction. Only concern yourself with the circumstances you create through your own decision-making as led by the Spirit. By doing so you will always be where God has determined for you to be and by continuously applying the Word in that place, you will allow the dominion of God's government to always have the last say, no matter the conditions of your present situation.

Kingdom Faith & Kingdom Paradigms

The image of God is not a *shape*, it is a way of thinking that *shapes* your life. It exists to perpetuate the lifestyle of His Blessing in the lives of those who seek Him and come into alignment with His thoughts. His thoughts are law, and they are also the most intimate part of Him. When we spend time adjusting to the principles of God's Kingdom we are actually seeking His heart. The more we seek His heart the more He reveals His purpose and His law designed for us to live out of. This is what I call Kingdom faith.

The image of God is not a *shape*, it is a way of thinking that *shapes* your life.

The image of God is not a *shape*, it is a way of thinking that *shapes* your life.

Kingdom faith means that based on God's original concept and intent of His promises you are constantly taking some type of action to see His divine laws manifested in your physical reality. It also means that as you exchange negative concepts for Kingdom truth, the beauty of God's intention begins to unfold and gradually you will begin to conform to His purpose. Kingdom Faith is not rational, reasonable, or emotional; it hears & obeys with consistency, and it produces favorable conditions for His Word to be manifested in the believer's life. Every one of God's promises has unique value, and adjusting your heart to that value will always inspire you to action. And the key to manifesting the Kingdom is constant movement. What can you do today to ensure that God's laws & His promises are in active perpetuation in your life?

The quality of God's promises gives us intrinsic value. The more we understand that we are created out of those intimate thoughts and unique purposes of God Himself, we will begin to see ourselves with a renewed perspective and in His light. Based on the light of that new truth, those unique and valuable promises will forever change how we view ourselves. It is then our job to live out of that unique change called a Kingdom paradigm. Kingdom faith will always lead to a Kingdom paradigm. A Kingdom paradigm happens when an old way of thinking dies and as a result of that new concept, a new season emerges.

When a Kingdom paradigm takes place you function completely in that new truth because the old mindset is no longer active. Another way to describe this paradigm is by the word "shift." God's next move in your life will always be preceded by an internal shift that takes place. Without the shift, God's plan cannot be fully grasped, leading to seasonal delay. God cannot increase any area of your life until He has shifted you there. Many people are afraid of being shifted because it involves being stretched and taking on a new mindset. As a result real breakthrough rarely occurs in their life.

Think of it this way, a butterfly cannot recall its caterpillar days, because it has no memory of that life. It has experienced a dramatic *shift*, thus it has died to that way of life and gone through real transformation. When a Kingdom truth impacts an individual's philosophy and thinking, they should never go back to that same way of thinking. When they do, they give permission to the limitations of the cursed world lifestyle to govern them again. Look at Colossians 2:20:

> *[Since you died to Christ with the basic principles of this world, why, as though you still belonged to it do you submit to its laws?]*

The "basic principles of this world" can also be understood as "basic patterns." Referring back to the Gestalt Learning Theory, scientific studies confirmed that our brain activity functions in patterns. So again, everything we do is the result of a thought pattern we have and those thought patterns create behaviors that will determine our quality of life. God's desire, through a new Kingdom mindset, is to fully and completely exchange your limited concept of life for His unlimited thought power. That power is designed to help us understand that nothing about the Word ever says failure or defeat, which means every season of life is really another door of opportunity to experience an increased measure of grace and abundance.

If you win in your mind, you will win in life. You are a victory waiting to happen. Though life has its way of replaying the negative outcomes of life over and over, it doesn't mean that is going to be your end. God gave you an expected end (Jeremiah 29:11) and it's released in a greater measure every time you successfully adjust to more of His thoughts and promises.

If you win in your mind, you will win in life. You are a victory waiting to happen.

> **If you win in your mind, you will win in life. You are a victory waiting to happen.**

Some Power Concepts for Your Thought Life:

1. Drawing from the substance of Christ's thought life.

    *   I have the mind of Christ.
    *   The Life of Christ flows within me.
    *   Since Christ is not limited, neither am I.

2. Choosing your source depends on what you think.

    *   Ideas that limit how I think are sourced with the curse.
    *   Thoughts that flow from the Blessing always empower and encourage me to follow my dreams.
    *   God will never tell me something is impossible or that I can't accomplish it.

3. You have the power to change concepts.

    *   Thoughts and ideas organize to become concepts.
    *   To change a negative concept into a positive one, I must rearrange the thoughts and ideas that influence my perception.
    *   As my concepts are changing I am changing, my life is changing and my destiny is changing.

4. The power to change your reality is in what you say and think.

    *   My thoughts are the source of my existence.
    *   My thoughts will naturally transform into tangible energy through my words.
    *   The words I am speaking are literally reshaping my world.

5. The power to live above limitations.

   - I can exchange limited thoughts with unlimited imagination of Jesus.
   - My thought power always gives me some say over my situation.
   - If I am able to think it, I have the divine ability to achieve it.

6

Power Concepts II: Embracing the Kingdom Concept

"The human mind, once stretched by a new idea, never regains its original dimensions." — Oliver Wendell Holmes

The Seed of Thought

The idea of concepts is so powerful that it only takes the seed of an idea to create an entirely new philosophy. The most popular religions and powerful movements all originated from the seed of thoughts and ideas. Remember that Adam became subject to a fallen paradigm that he perpetuated by entertaining a tiny seed concept: *that he was not made in the image and likeness of God.*

As I mentioned previously, once Adam accepted that idea or seed, a new garden began to spring forth and eventually he began to cultivate it leading to an entire paradigm shift in how he viewed himself, life, and God. In order to be effective with thought training we need to understand how powerful the concepts we believe really are.

In the same sense, Jesus said the Kingdom of Heaven was the same concept of sowing a seed. Why? Because that seed of a Kingdom paradigm will grow to influence every arena of your life as long as you cultivate it with the right things. You must understand how the Kingdom operates and that everything God does is like seed He is planting. Don't despise small beginnings; understand the seed concept and that God is getting ready to release something big in your life.

This makes the importance of gaining a Kingdom paradigm all the more important. Thoughts can change the world around us just by cultivating our perceptions to see and expect things a certain way. However, what I have found is that seed, or an originating concept, cannot live within us or even take root unless we have set the atmosphere for it to grow. A seed cannot grow in shallow ground. No matter how good that seed is, it will die off. The same way the land has to be prepared for seed to grow, our minds must be positioned and groomed to take in and receive new truth that can radically change us. If we don't cultivate a Kingdom paradigm our chances of making an impact with God's government will quickly wither away.

For example, doubt can only come in and live if we have created an atmosphere for it. Telling doubt to leave won't work if we've made a comfortable living arrangement for it in the space of our hearts. Jesus said that when a spirit is cast out it comes back to see if there is still room for it to live. What are you making room for in your mind? Are you allowing a constant flow of life-generating concepts to envelope you and cultivate the perceptions of the King? Are you embracing the change God is trying to bring forth in you by allowing His mind to dominate yours? You must set the right atmosphere, embrace the change, and prepare to let go of every thought, idea, belief, and paradigm you hold onto that doesn't prosper your soul and your life.

As your concepts change and you exchange your thought life with God's thought life, the new you will begin to emerge on a greater level and dimension. Prepare to make room for the new you that's about to break forth. The Kingdom of God in you is about to leak out into every area of your life.

JUMP: a Concept for Embracing the New

Success in life will come faster the sooner we are willing to let go of old ways, philosophies, and habits. The longer we remain stuck in traditional thinking and unproductive perceptions, the more we hinder the enormous and rich destiny that awaits us.

That's because your new life needs room. One of the core driving points of the Kingdom is that it exists to expand or seize more territory. That means the Kingdom is ever enlarging and increasing. Simply put, if you want to have a new and successful lifestyle, you are going to have to "make room" for it. You are going to have to create space to receive new truth, new ideas, and new strategies for achieving the things you want in life.

The most important question is: How do you begin to make room for this new life to emerge? How do you break free from those old ideas and philosophies so that they never hold you captive again? How do you follow through in that new truth to create lasting change? Let's look at another Kingdom principle called "advancement" to answer those questions.

Enlarging your destiny means enlarging your territory. Committing yourself to becoming a person driven by destiny and inner purpose is really opening your heart to radical change that will eventually take you where you want to be. By doing this you are increasing your capacity to receive new truth. This is where the "new you" and your successful life begin to emerge. A powerful and successful you that has always been there waiting to be unleashed given the right space needed.

You see, in a Kingdom every territorial expansion begins with the invasion of another province or city. This means that good thoughts, great ideas, and new belief systems are trying to invade your heart with powerful practices to position you for greater success. You were created to have practical solutions and the right perspective on everyday life. Many people limit the good that wants to break forth by limiting their spiritual experience to just four walls. Always remember that God's plan for you is much bigger than four walls and that plan is to produce real prosperity in every realm of your life.

When the "new life within" invades your territory there is a radical thought change, a paradigm shift that takes place and the former way of thinking becomes obsolete. You are making room for the new by moving out the old. The key to breaking free from the confines of old ideas and unleashing this invasion of a successful you is: you have to JUMP!

Jumping means that you let go of old ideas, concepts, and relationships, whatever feeds the old you, by completely immersing yourself into the new that's in front of you!

If you are going to enlarge your destiny you need to prepare for change. From here on out prepare for things to radically shift your perceptions and your way of doing things. Expect it, accept it, and agree with the change. Completely release yourself to fall freely into the new and unstoppable you within that's about to emerge.

The Law of Immersion

You know, the concept of the Kingdom being within you is simple: you have and possess everything you need to create the life you want now. All of its power, authority, and potential have been available to each and every individual if they're willing to submit to the change that will eventually bring forth their new and unlimited life from within. Think about that, the power to fulfill every dream, live in increase and abundance, along with a fail-proof plan, has always been standing right within your reach.

As I stated earlier, every great change needs to begin with space or room being made to receive the new. So leading up to the time of Jesus' arrival, a powerful man emerged in the earth named John, who taught one simple principle along with the Kingdom message: "baptism." John would baptize or "dip" people in the water as they received the Kingdom. However, the meaning was much more significant than many believers often realize.

Baptism is "baptizo" in Greek and it means to dip or immerse. What is important for you to know is that the key to unlocking the richness that is within you is first completely immersing yourself in new principles and ideas. You have to become a student of change.

I am convinced that many individuals today are still frustrated with their experience of life materially and spirituality because they fail to completely entrust themselves to the right path and change needed to really produce results. The principle about immersion is simple: you have to fully commit and submit yourself to any new truth or principle in order to truly experience the entire impact of that new reality.

Jumping is never about who or what you're leaving behind, it's always about the new that is breaking forth.

Again, jumping is completely immersing yourself in the new that wants to break forth in your life. Jumping is never about who or what you're leaving behind, it's always about the new that is breaking forth. This means you let go of the old to embrace your purpose and destiny. It means you dive both feet into the new that's waiting for you, without a life jacket or parachute, you are prepared to fully embrace the new that your successful life is bringing forth within you. This means you are giving yourself over to a new plan and system, ultimately shaping a greater and more abundant destiny. What are you waiting for?

Jump! That is exactly what you need to do in order to fully access, embrace, and experience the Kingdom in a tangible way.

The law of immersion is simple: whatever you give yourself to, it will give itself back in a greater measure. Many people are familiar with the scripture verse, *"Give and it will be given unto you, pressed down shaken together and running over"* (Luke 6:38). The principle here is: what you are not willing to give yourself over to will not give itself back to you.

Many Christians fail to see the amazing potential that they could possess because they are so unwilling to deeply embrace the Kingdom philosophy in life. They aren't ready and willing to embrace a new way of doing things, and quite frankly the thought and idea of change terrifies them. However, change requires investment. What you sow you will reap, but how consistent are you in investing the change you desire to see?

There isn't anyone successful today that didn't totally commit to change. What you are willing to invest into the change will pay rewarding dividends, but you can't bring forth the new holding onto the old. You have to depart from older paradigms and invest into the new that God wants to unleash in you. This is functioning in the law of immersion and is guaranteed to release an authentic Kingdom experience as you engage its meaning and concept.

Operating in the immersion principle means:

- You aren't afraid of change and new growth.
- You have committed to the change breaking forth.
- You choose your relationships based on that change and new direction.
- You are consistent in new principles and thoughts.
- You do not give up quickly when applying a new way of life. You must remain consistent in thought and application.

- You rehearse and spend time with every new principle. The same goes if you adopt new philosophies to run your business, strategies to enhance your leadership, or conflict resolution tactics. Immersion means you embrace the new philosophy and rehearse it daily to see results with it.
- You believe and totally trust there is a successful life within you. You allow that successful life to come forth by committing to its manifestations.
- You are willing to walk away from any person, place, or influence that doesn't push you in the direction of your success plan and destiny driven life.
- You are letting go of the old and choosing to fully accept and embrace the new that's right in front of you.
- You recognize the old beliefs and patterns that haven't brought forth fruit in your life, and you are ready to make room in order to change them.

Parachute Complex

A common misperception in life is that "God will do it for me." Some believe, "If I want it bad enough things will work themselves out." Others think, "Things will just fall into place somehow." All of these perceptions are wrong and have left many individuals frustrated in life and their spiritual experience because they aren't applying any new action to what they believe.

The truth is, our lives are a sum total of what we believe, decide and the course of action we are willing to take in any situation to see those belief systems manifest. Life must be embraced just as any change must be embraced as well. This means you are willing to take action to see the new change emerge.

Things are always subject to change with one courageous act of faith or positive declaration. However, we have to believe this. We have to be truly convinced that we have the last say in our own lives and no one else is responsible for our outcomes but us. What we allow will happen. When we leave things in our lives up for grasp with negative words and defeated mentalities, negative forces and oppositions will eventually overcome them.

It's time for a change. It's time for an attitude adjustment. It's time to just "let go." It can be hard to adopt new ways of thinking, especially when we have believed and thought one way for a very long time. Whether we realize it or not we become intimate with our ideas and belief systems. We become accustomed to what seems "right and comfortable" even if what we think isn't necessarily the best thing for us. Once we have committed to a certain way of thinking, changing those thought patterns can have a great frustrating and alarming impact.

Many individuals feel somewhat "violated" when things they were taught by their mother, father, or grandparents becomes challenged with new truth. That's understandable. For most of us, as children growing up, in our eyes our parents can do no wrong. We trust them unconditionally and believe with our whole hearts what they tell us. That is the natural function of a child's heart; it is innocent and submissive. However, you cannot allow old paradigms to hinder your "jump" or to cause you to hold back from unleashing yourself in the change that's happening. You can't half-heartedly embrace change and expect real results. I call it the "parachute complex." When people have a parachute mentality they tend to fear change or try to find the most comfortable way to experience change. When you "jump" into change, there is no safe landing!

When you fully embrace God's change and the new He is bringing forth don't try to soften the land with logic, reasoning or excuses. Leap into your destiny because the less concerned with comfort you are, the more speed and momentum you build on your way into breakthrough change. You are gaining acceleration through expectation and concentration on the change no matter how it may come. That acceleration is going to create an impact of change that will cause you to never be the same.

As you are gaining a mental picture of the radical change God wants to break forth in you, you may realize by now, that in your reality a big jump with no parachute could most likely end your life. That's exactly what this change or a Kingdom experience is intended to do: put an end to the old you and force the new life in you to automatically emerge. Remember that we can only be transformed by renewing our mind (Romans 12:22). This is the jump concept. We must change our mind in order to experience total transformation. In that transformation process something dies. Just like a caterpillar transforms, but when it crosses the threshold of change it becomes a butterfly and can never return to its caterpillar days no matter how hard it tries. That's real change, when the old passes away and all things become new (2 Corinthians 5:22).

So you see, you can't afford to have a parachute complex when embracing real Kingdom change. Otherwise you'll hinder the breakthrough, delay change and block your turnaround. Let yourself go and allow permanent change to bring you across the threshold of a new identity and reality in the sovereign Kingdom of Jesus. That's why Jesus didn't preach the Kingdom without preaching "repent!" Repentance again, is change. He knew in order to change your life, you have to change your mind which means you have to "jump" into a whole new world governed by the principles and purposes of God's unlimited creativity.

Breaking Free from the Parachute

In order to break free from a parachute complex we have to realize how deeply embedded in us certain ideas and thought patterns are because we've believed them our entire lives and they stay the same unless we decide to change them. In fact, science proves that none of us are born with a particular language programmed in our brains. That means if I were to grow up with a Spanish speaking family, although I am African American, I would speak Spanish fluently rather than English. This is because everything we do, say, like and believe is a result of being learned. We are taught to think and speak based on our cultures and the environments we grow up in.

Similarly, none of us are programmed with a favorite color, we learned that too. Neither do we come out of the womb with a favorite food in mind; this too was taught to us through an experience of some kind. What I want to impress upon you is the importance of understanding how deeply imbedded our philosophies, ideas and ways are within us. We have to realize we were taught through emotional experiences or something we've seen, heard or watched over and over again. Rehearsal is the number one way we learn and retain something.

This creates an intimacy with what has flown from our previous experience, environments and belief systems to us, and many of us want to hold onto them forever. However, I want to ask you: What do you do when what you have believed for so long is the thing keeping you from what you've desired to achieve for so long? Take a moment to really think about that. I want to challenge you to take the mask off, be straight forward, and be honest with yourself. How have those old belief systems you've held onto pushed you into your destiny? How have they actually created opportunities of success for you? You'll find that some have, because not all that we have learned has been bad for us, and that certainly isn't my intention of expression. However, you will also realize that much of what you were taught hasn't propelled you into victory in your life.

What do you do when what you have believed for so long is the thing keeping you from what you've desired to achieve for so long?

My transformational experience in life came as a result of my encounter with new truth and the reality that I had been functioning in misperceptions my whole life. My greatest change experience came when I was first confronted with the idea that what I had been taught about life, success and making things happen most of my life growing up were potentially wrong.

Believe me, at first I wasn't willing to embrace this change, let alone make room for new truth. I mean, the idea was absolutely shocking, uncomfortable and irritating to me that I believed so many lies. At first I didn't want to believe it. I just knew that everything I learned in church growing up had to be right! I mean, it's church, right? It has to all be correct. I just knew that all the Sunday school lessons and sermons we ever learned were exactly right! I was fully convinced that whatever grandmother and grandfather taught us about God and life had to be right, because well, they are "granny and grandma!"

I was intimate with my belief systems, even the toxic views I had toward life and achievement. I was comfortable in my ignorance until I began to challenge my religious reasoning by simply doing one thing: comparing what I had been believing with the results I was getting in my everyday life. It was plain as day. I was beginning to realize even though I was a "Christian" I was always depressed, lacking and frustrated in life. I wasn't happy in my relationship with God, I was miserable. I didn't know who God really was, I didn't understand my purpose in life, and I was constantly questioning if God was really there and whether or not He really hears prayers! You may be able to relate.

I noticed that for some reason I was always afraid of God and wondering when He was going to punish me next for all the bad things I had done in my life. I was in total fear and captivity, not in love with my Creator. I finally accepted the idea that this could be wrong. What I had been taught growing up didn't ingrain the perspective of God's love into me; it filled me with fear of Him. I found myself often wondering when God was going to strike and repay me for all of my sins! I know that sounds crazy and even a little funny, but if we are honest this is the experience of most Christians today.

Although it was painful at first to accept the idea that God and life were much bigger than what I had been seeing, and that much of the teaching I got about Him was wrong, I eventually began to adjust to the internal transition that was taking place within me, and I changed my inner picture of life.

The defining characteristic of real change is that it is spiritual and therefore you cannot see it with your physical eyesight. That means whatever is breaking forth within you is going to require faith to manifest and experience it. It also means that you are going to need patience as the entire transition comes to full fruition. By strategically and instrumentally using these principles, ideas, and concepts, give way to gradually changing those toxic thoughts and belief systems that have hindered you and held you back. By getting rid of those old habits, you empower the new you, perspective, and thought life. You must keep in mind though, that transitioning into your new life and way of thinking can be uncomfortable and a little rocky as you begin to learn how to use faith to experience change, and ultimately making your destiny a tangible reality. Your faith will give you the strength you need to endure the pressure of changing your mindset and breaking out of the limitations that have surrounded you.

You have to be willing to interrupt your intimacy with those erroneous thought patterns you have about life and what you are able to achieve, just as I did. Prepare to replace them and create a new intimacy of thought in you, an intimacy with good and empowering thoughts, ideas, and belief structures. In order to make this adjustment you have to be willing to confront the ideas that aren't producing fruit in your life, no matter how long you've held onto them, and abandon those old ideas for the incoming richness of an abundant thought life.

Is it possible that some of what you have believed concerning relationships, leadership and life are wrong? Could those bad belief systems be producing unfavorable conditions for you? Many people go through divorce because of what they call "irreconcilable differences." However, many really just failed to undo some bad philosophies they were taught about marriage and relationships. Think about that. Many leaders are not poor leaders; they just need to adjust their philosophies no matter how long they've held on to them.

Make the decision to open your heart completely and make room for new ideas and thoughts to invade your life. Don't be afraid of change. Be confident in knowing there is always a plan and a vision within you that is greater than you can ever imagine. Remember that in order to attain that vision, there will have to be changes and mental adjustments. Remind yourself that in order to get what you have never had, you have to do what you've never done.

When you think this way, you are making space for the new you to emerge. You are giving Him room to invade your spiritual and personal territory with new laws and principles to govern your life. This opens the doors to greatness and untapped potential you didn't even know was inside of you. One of the ways I was able to get free from my old thinking habits and religious philosophies was through a committed and determined faith to tap into all the richness that was inside of me. Focusing on the greatness that is about to emerge will help you remain keen and in alignment with the change breaking forth in you.

Remember that the purpose of focus is to accelerate change in you and break your mind out of any boundaries that exist against the immense vision and plan that exists for your life. You cannot experience the change without accepting and completely focusing on the new that is about to break forth. Many individuals block the good that wants to emerge in their lives, trapped by old mindsets, stubborn and unfruitful thinking with no real intention of fully focusing and embracing change.

As a result, most of the time they lose the change that was beginning to emerge. That new and successful mindset needs time, faith, encouragement, commitment, and most of all faith. And that territory begins in your heart. You have to make room by letting go of old ideas. You don't have fear or worry about losing intimacy with old ways, a new and more strategic and successful you is about to come forth once you choose to let them go!

Only as I opened my heart to this change did I begin to experience a world and realm that I never knew existed. I began to experience the Kingdom reality and my life has never been the same.

An incredible change is about to take place in your life as you open yourself to the abundant thoughts, ideas and strategies of a total victorious you on the inside waiting to be unleashed. You are engaging in a personal thought exchange with your new self. You'll have the opportunity to see the invisible, think with an elevated mindset, and leverage those concepts into victorious living strategies for your everyday life!

Cultivating the New

Immersing yourself in the new that wants to break forth in you creates the opportunity and space you need to make radical changes and embrace a new reality and destiny. As you totally shift your way of thinking, the new and capable you will increase territory in the terrain of your heart with a constant flow of new ideas, philosophies and life strategies.

There is no doubt that God wants to produce His culture within you. His intention is that you, as His "image," will reflect the same culture back into this world and positively impact it with lasting change. If you're not careful, that change can be lost if you fail to cultivate the new "you" that is emerging in the midst of this radical shift taking place.

When cultivating the Kingdom reality, clarity is extremely important. Clarity is the ability to look into a matter and perceive its purpose and reason. Based on the purpose one is able to discern where something fits in their life, or if it fits at all for that matter. Things that "fit" in our lives always support where we are headed and the direction of our destiny. Fitting also implies that force is not needed. As one is operating out of the endless flow of agreement with a divine plan, a natural "fit" comes as a result of divine appointment.

Clarity is the ability to determine what fits and what does not in your life based on the season you are in. Do you understand what season you are in? Life is lived in seasons, and clarity gives you the ability to look into that season and discern perfectly its purpose and the plan of God for it.

This is one of the functions of clarity: the ability to correctly perceive and benefit from a season. The emergence and expansion of your new life exists to give you clarity in all matters. It is important for you to see life through the eyes of faith, truth and hope, clear and definite. This state of clarity increases peace of mind and settles the confusion that everyday life and chaos try to bring. Clarity makes it harder to be distracted and increases your overall performance and results in life.

When we make decisions based on the clarity of our inner purpose we design an endless path of positive flow leading us into open doors and the right direction for our life.

When people and things come into our life and disrupt the flow of positive energy and the direction

When we make decisions based on the clarity of our inner purpose we design an endless path of positive flow leading us into open doors and the right direction for our life.

we are headed, we can easily tell they don't "fit" because we are functioning out of a momentous flow created by the new thought life and change in decision making have set us on. As a result you can shamelessly pass up relationships that don't "feel right." A clicking is absent because that person has not been divinely sent into your life. This is the power of clarity. When we make decisions based on the clarity of our inner purpose we design an endless path of positive flow leading us into open doors and the right direction for our life.

Creating clarity begins with focus. Focus means you narrow in on the purpose and reason for something and are constantly making decisions to move you in that same destiny. You need to be clear about what you want out of life. Then you need to be clear about what steps you are willing to take to make it happen. This all begins with focus.

You have to decide season by season what matters most and what you will zero in on. Make sure you are making every moment count by deciding to only fill your time with what matters most to you. This focus always creates clarity and brings the plan of God into greater harmony in your life.

Clarity also creates natural emergence. As you gain greater focus, you will be in greater harmony with your destiny and plan. From that plan, untapped gifts, talents, and creativity will begin to emerge. Without trying, you will be unlocking a greater you as your destiny is intended to do just that. As you commit to leading a focused life, you are positioning yourself to experience a new and richer you! Take the time to dedicate yourself to a life of clarity.

Clarity will always cause you to make better decisions with greater speed and accuracy. The faster you can look into a thing and decide whether or not it fits in your life, the faster and greater you will emerge and the more successful you can become, creating a more prosperous and meaningful life.

You have to keep in mind that God's intention for you flows from a NOW state. Remember that you have to "keep step with Him," meaning that growth will increase and quickly bring about change. Clearly defined goals are needed NOW. Focus is needed NOW.

Relationship discernment is needed NOW. Faith is needed NOW. The now mindset helps to cultivate the new you that is emerging through God's heavenly system.

The Now Message

Did you know that you were intimately created with detail long before you were born? You were created with destiny on your plate before the foundations of life were even laid! Before the existence of all creation and the formation of all creatures, you were being built, designed and orchestrated with a plan to create the most enjoyable life possible. That can only mean one thing: what God has in store for you, He wants to get over to you, now! Think about it.

God was so excited to give Himself to you that He started fellowshipping with you in His thoughts. That's why He knew you before you were formed in your mother's womb. God has always been excited about you and thrilled about His purpose and plan for you.

Have you ever been so excited to go some place that you were up and dressed hours before it was time to be there? I have. At times the excitement and anticipation of something so great can drive us to begin taking some action towards it just to suffice for the adrenaline rush we have. God was so excited about your arrival and existence into planet earth that He began secret and intimate communication with you before you were actually here.

The more you understand this, the bigger the picture of life becomes, because you will now see how great the expectation for your life is and what it should be to you. The plan is to heal you now. Be Blessed now. Be prosperous now, increase now, and break through now! Not tomorrow, not next week or next year; there's something new that wants to break forth in you now! God didn't get such a jump-start on your creation just to get you here and then place pauses and delays in your life. He wants you to live out of a "now" reality. He wants you to know you can overcome every delay and hindrance with the right information and principles applied. A popular scripture verse (Matthew 6:13) says it plainly:

["For the Kingdom, the power and glory are yours now and forever."]

As you are totally embracing the reality of the Kingdom concept you must understand the principle and the power of the now concept. The Kingdom model doesn't have a time calendar attached to it, because it originates and exists outside of the boundaries of time. That means not only is it practical to expect something now, but it is also your divine right to believe that things can turn around for you at any time on any given day.

That is what makes the unlimited you inside so powerful. It doesn't have regards for the limitations of life. You may be facing some pressing circumstances and it may seem your deliverance is far away. Don't think that way. You have to press the delete button on every thought that causes things to seem as though your breakthrough and dreams are too far out of reach.

This kind of thinking can cause mental exhaustion and makes an individual feel as though they are limited to the time system of their current struggle. If you allow time to discourage you, you'll begin measuring your breakthrough with how long you've been going through. Stop watching the clock, realize the unlimited you has enough power inside to change things now, if you are willing to accept it. No one can schedule your breakthrough accept you.

Press delete. Clear and erase your mind of every defeated thought that comes to add pressure to your faith. Don't let it exhaust you. You are about to change things now. You can expect things to turn around immediately if you are willing act on it, no matter how crazy it may seem. Trust that now is your season to prosper, and be empowered to experience endless victory.

One of the ways to tap into this now reality is to be willing to take courageous steps of faith. Don't be hindered by what seems logical because faith doesn't demand logic, it demands trust, hope, and vision. If you can see it, you most certainly can possess it. This is the power of vision. Act now. Go for it.

Having a Personal Exchange with God

Making an exchange with God begins in the mind and heart and is an important key when grasping the extension of His overall Kingdom lifestyle. Blueprints to power paths are laid out, but are only revealed the more and more we wake up the unlimited God nature within us. You see, God's intent is that through His sovereign will and divine principles you will have every solution to life's problems. He wants to exchange His reality for yours through divine problem solving, strategic planning and great decision-making. Again God doesn't just want to exchange thoughts with you, He wants to exchange His life with you. That is why Jesus "gave up His life" so that you could draw from every benefit of His divine nature.

Exchanging with God is useful in every area of life, not just spiritual ones. Leading, running a business, and organizing all require healthy philosophies and strategic principles that best guarantee the future success of any establishment.

Imagine how much more successful you could be in leadership or managing your company if you had the perspective of the King to influence all of your decisions. When you exchange with God, this is what happens. There are no limits and boundaries to your access to God's abundant supply of ideas, strategies, and concepts. You have the legal right, as an heir to His Kingdom, to access even the most intimate parts of Him!

Many leaders in faith-based organizations are unsuccessful in leading because they fail to exchange their belief systems with God's when it comes to every person, matter and situation in their company. You can become quickly frustrated with leading an organization when you fail to realize that "believing in God" doesn't always mean you have the same "beliefs as God." The Kingdom is total access to God's belief systems.

You see, the same way God has to transform our lives by renewing our perspective about Him is the same way we have to create change in our personal lives, businesses, and relationships. Just because we have the Kingdom doesn't mean we automatically understand God's perspective of leadership.

We have to strategically yield to God's idea of leading, as in every area of our life, in order to have thought exchange with Him. We must do this continually until we enter into an endless of flow of His ideas in that particular area. An endless flow marks the point in which you become in perfect harmony and agreement with the principles of God, creating a continuous exchange of God's thoughts with yours and leveraging them to produce His authentic arrangements in your business, personal life, and relationships.

Begin to let God know that you desire an endless flow of His ideas in your relationship with Him. Incorporate this prayer into your daily confession: "God, I believe I have an endless flow of your ideas and perspectives and I am in agreement with them."

You may be the leader of a company or organization, the executive of a large corporation, or the owner of a small business. Regardless of your position you need to tap into God's endless flow of life-generating thoughts to experience optimal performance in your personal and professional areas of life. Let go of what isn't working and tap into the Kingdom supply. Tapping into God's Kingdom for His divine insights will create that constant exchange you need to accelerate your path to success. As you overcome the pain of your change, you will soon notice you are creating consistent flow in God's ideas and agreement along with increasing your overall quality of life, leadership, and relationship building.

Breaking Attachments

I want you to think about something for a moment: you are the sum total of the people around you. Every relationship is like a proton that generates more energy into your life. If you're willing to break the attachments of negative people around you the overall energy of your life will shift, ultimately changing what you attract to yourself.

Old relationships can interrupt your exchange with God. Don't let this happen. Remember, valuing your destiny is the key to breaking off people who should not be in your life. The more value you place on your life, the more value you will place on your time. The more value you place on your time, the more unwilling you will be to allow people to waste it with negativity and lack of support.

Don't allow the negative energy of guilt and shame to keep you from separating yourself from relationships that are toxic to your divine destiny. You can love people from a distance. You can check in on them every now and then. However, you have to keep in mind you are flowing with God and nothing can interrupt that. You have too much to gain and too much destiny within you. As you move out the people who shouldn't be in your life, you are making room for God to bring in the people that should be there.

7

Grace to Succeed:
Your Winning Potential

" . . . those who receive overflowing grace (unmerited favor)
and the free gift of righteousness will reign as kings in life . . ."
(Romans 5:17)

Grace, the Unlimited Potential

The common hindrance most Christians often experience is not knowing how truly valuable they are to God. It seems that for years in the church religious teaching has been centered on what believers are not doing right, instead of what they are capable of doing! The Kingdom of Heaven is not a "what you're doing wrong" concept. Yet, there are many sermons reminding people of how sinful they are and how much God hates sin. This should not be the core of any ministry's message.

Though it is important that people understand God's expectation for their lifestyle, sin-conscious preaching cannot be at the core of the Gospel message. If it is, then it is only reinforcing to Christians how limited they are. That is why Christ preached the Kingdom, not a sin-conscious message reminding people of their limitations. The Kingdom is a message of possibility and hope beyond all odds. It is God's modus and tool given to us in order that we might experience the richness of His increase despite our limited sinful nature.

The Kingdom encompasses all of God's power and unlimited ability that flows from His throne of Grace into our heart to lift us above the gravity of a limited mindset. Though your eyes cannot see it, you are currently standing in the glory, majesty, splendor, and power of that throne right now! That Grace is your empowering source to break free mentally and succeed every time. Romans 5:1-2:

> *[Therefore, since we have been justified through faith, we have peace with God through our Lord Jesus Christ, through whom we have gained access by faith into this grace in which we now stand.]*

One of the reasons you are so valuable to God is because He's endowed you with so much of His "Grace." Hebrews 4:16 encourages to us have confidence concerning God's Grace in us:

> *[Let us then approach God's throne of grace with confidence, so that we may receive mercy and find grace to help us in our time of need.]*

Grace is favor. Grace is divine enablement and the authentic power of Christ's complete and unlimited reign within us. It is God's supernatural strength downloaded to us through His precious Holy Spirit. It is God's gift to us, the strength of His Grace is literally a divine ability to overcome and thrive in every sphere of life.

Grace doesn't end there though. Grace is the power to possess. Grace exceeds human potential and allows you to rise above the normal limitations of your natural capabilities. It is God's divine energy that flows from the manifested and actual existence of His supernatural throne within us. That divine Grace is translated to us through the release of anointing, which comes through a real experience and encounter with God's Spirit. That same Spirit strengthens us with His internal Kingship, making us automatic co-heirs or joint heirs with Christ and all the full benefits of His divine contracts.

The more consistent we become in our awareness of these divine benefits, the more we can place a legal demand on them and remain in continuous expectation that at any moment we can exercise Heaven's benefits to influence our reality.

Greater Clarity of Grace

The definition of Grace can be wrongly understood because it is used so many different ways in the Bible. However, I strongly believe that one of the keys to unleashing God's Grace in greater dimensions is by gaining better clarity and understanding of what Grace is and learning exactly how it functions in our personal lives.

Keep in mind Grace has been used at times to express favor, or speaking favorably. Other times it's used to express the unlimited love, kindness and compassion of God. All of these are true. While there has been much debate over these definitions in the church, the truth is that Grace encompasses a wide range of spiritual benefits that one receives as a result of the gift of the divine presence of God, the King, flowing in their life. Grace means favor, abundance, prosperity, wholeness, and completeness as well, and all of these flow from the throne of Heaven into the heart of every believer. Whether you know it or not, you have been endowed with His splendor and the glory of His majesty. This is the presence of His royalty flowing within you that makes you a king, fit to rule in God's Kingdom.

The presence of Grace dismisses you from all of your sin and previous failures. It only takes into account God's enabling power giving you the divine strength to overcome each and every one of your flaws. Yes, Grace abounds where sin does, but not so that people may have a license to live immorally. Grace abounds so that the strength within you continually gives you the power to overcome those limitations that keep showing up in your life.

With this in mind, I like to think of Grace as the divine energy of the King hidden in the capsule of His Word. That Word, when it is understood and acted upon is power for releasing divine healing, prosperity, and supernatural wealth. Grace empowers you to receive all these things! It leaves nothing out. It includes all of the benefits of God's favor, mercy, love, compassion, and kindness. Grace is the full package of God's Blessing, and He supplies all of your needs through the unlimited riches of His wisdom, power, glory, and strength.

Grace is the full package of God's Blessing, and He supplies all of your needs through the unlimited riches of His wisdom, power, glory, and strength.

> Grace is the full package of God's Blessing, and He supplies all of your needs through the unlimited riches of His wisdom, power, glory, and strength.

So when God's supernatural power flows through you, think of it as grace moving, doing what it was designed and purposed to do. Be encouraged knowing that God our King, who sits on the throne, was intentional about endowing you with every ounce of that empowering Grace. That very power releases untapped potential and equips us to experience a winner's mentality and lifestyle regardless of the season we find ourselves in. In this regard, Grace is the power and strength to gain the competitive advantage in every situation and nothing less. It always positions you for the most favorable outcome.

The more conscious of this this revelation of Grace we become the more we began to hear the gentle voice of victory constantly reminding us that "losing is not an option." I believe it's there, within us all, if we choose to listen and concentrate on the divine strength within us through God's Grace, we'll always be conscious of our winning potential. Therefore, you aren't simply graced to win you are graced to win and win big!

Grace's Unlimited Benefits

[Let us therefore come boldly unto the throne of grace that we may obtain mercy, and find grace to help in time of need.]

Here we see that we also receive mercy from God's (throne of) Grace. Mercy isn't to be confused with Grace. Paul expresses that mercy is available as a result of God's throne "of Grace" and presence in our life. He then says as a result of that throne we can "find Grace" to help in a time of need. That "Grace" Paul was referring to this time was an endowment of mercy, nonetheless he calls mercy a particular Grace or empowerment you can access as a result of God's throne existing in you. Paul was simply expressing Grace as your mercy. What does that mean? It means that mercy is another benefit that we inherit as heirs to God's Kingdom and His entire estate.

You see, since we have been given all the benefits of the Kingdom, nothing can be left out. That's why the passage encourages us to come with "boldness" when we talk to God. This is confidence, not arrogance. It's an attitude, an attitude of Kings. On the Ark of the Covenant, the "mercy" seat is representational of the place "Christ" is seated on as our ultimate sacrifice for sin. God's throne supplies us mercy or an endowment to receive whatever we need. God is saying to us: "Be confident." He has given us full access to His throne and provision for every time of need. Know your value when communicating with God. God wants us to take His provision and take His Grace (not ask for it), as He is standing at the throne freely handing it to us. To not be confident and bold about being participants of His divine empowerment is to relinquish the internal power inside that has the potential to produce the results we want out of life. Think about that, being timid about your position of power with Christ puts the overall quality of your life in jeopardy. Don't forfeit your power source, tap into unlimited Grace by shifting your paradigm and taking a bolder perspective towards interacting with the King.

Take a more forceful attitude about putting a constant demand on all of the benefits, including mercy, that He's offered you. Soon, you should begin talking to God differently. Let God know you realize your worth and value to Him and you want to start putting a real demand on what He's freely given you. Speak with an attitude of confidence that there is nothing you desire that hasn't already been provided through the eternal and sufficient Grace of your Father. This attitude of God will cause things to conform to God's favor for you. That favor will change your inner picture and cause you to realize open doors that you didn't even know existed.

Spiritual Dynamite

Please understand that as dearly beloved children created and formed in the image and likeness of God, every single one of us possesses the hidden capacity to dominate and to live with His excellence. That "hidden capacity" I am referring to is commonly known as potential, which derives from the Latin word *potentia* meaning "power!" The Bible mentions this power in Acts 1:8:

> *[But when the Holy Spirit has come upon you, you will receive power!]*

Now the word "power" here is literally translated in the Greek, from which the Latin meaning also derives. It simply means "dynamis" (dun-a-mis) from which we get the word "dynamite" in English. Think about that. By His Spirit, Christ has impressed upon us His explosive tangible force! Whether or not we choose to release that potential inside can decide the quality of life we experience here on earth. God gives you His explosive power to literally break out every time someone tries to hinder you or say, "You can only go this far." The idea is that through His Kingdom of Grace you are strapped with spiritual dynamite, giving you the power to explode free from any limitations trying to be placed on you.

The Power of a Winning Mentality

If you're going to win at life you will need God's strategy, which will unleash God's power and greatness that is within you. The first step to doing this is recognizing God's empowering grace that is inside of you. It is a knowing and an intentional effort to keep this idea at the forefront of your thoughts: God's grace is your power source, His life flowing in you, and at any time you can draw from the well of His throne to break through. This is called recognizing your "winning potential." God's power within is a grace to succeed. Realize that God ALWAYS causes us to triumph! Always, no matter what! This means we are predestined to be champions in Christ Jesus. Once you become consciously aware of that winning grace within you, you can begin to create turn around in any season of life.

Now, maybe you don't feel like a champion, and the circumstances you are facing tend to dictate something contrary. Well, that's nothing new, since we are born in sin and shaped in iniquity (Psalm 51:5) it's no wonder we are always facing opposition. I don't believe that verse only means we are all born sinners. More so, I believe it's an indication that because of our sinful, weak, and limited nature, the odds are always being stacked against us. What others say about you or against you isn't important at all. What matters most is that you don't accept it, and refuse to fall victim to a defeated perspective of yourself.

God hasn't asked us to feel anything, so emotions can't be an excuse for giving up. God only asks us to believe, be, and do! Believe His Word, be complete (holy), and act on it! In other words, when it comes to the obstacles we face in life, He asks us to function like Him: don't be influenced by what you see, rather make the decision to operate in the empowering grace of His supernatural law within. Kingdom laws don't have emotion, they are certain and unchanging. This means no matter what difficulty or adversity you're faced with, as long as you are consistently applying God's Word in every situation, you are tapping into grace through faith, and operating outside any limitations of your emotions.

You can stand with confidence that a higher spiritual law is working for you and you've already succeeded! That law is power; it is supernatural energy operating on it's own to perform a task. That law is the "law of grace". Its constant presence within gives you the supernatural ability to create a shift regardless of your situation. You have the power for turnaround!

In God's grace, there is always a plan to succeed. There is always a strategy for creating the shift you need to get the things you want.

In God's grace, there is always a plan to succeed. There is always a strategy for creating the shift you need to get the things you want. You have to learn to rely on the grace, God's supernatural empowerment

> In God's grace, there is always a plan to succeed. There is always a strategy for creating the shift you need to get the things you want.

inside of you. Don't entertain stress, worry, or thoughts of fear. Make the declaration: "God's grace is on the inside of me and He's already given me a plan to succeed." By doing this you'll be increasing in your winning nature and gradually growing in the "grace" of God's strength in you. Look at 2 Peter 3:18:

> *[But continue to grow in the grace and knowledge of our Lord and Savior Jesus Christ.]*

Growing in the Grace of God's Truth

As mentioned previously, growing in God's grace requires a healthy understanding of your inner value. Every day you're faced with contradictions, obstacles or challenges that are set in place to minimize your self-worth. Don't allow life to devalue you.

Though many people struggle with reoccurring negative cycles in their lives, many fail to realize the source of their negative cycles. However, when they can (see) lay hold of the truth that their own negative self-image is the source of these cycles, this same truth gives them power to stop generating such cycles and obtain true breakthrough for creating favorable outcomes. God's grace is there to give you a new image of who you are, to help you see that you are truly His reflection and regardless of what you've been through, a life of beauty on the inside is still within you waiting to be unleashed.

It's easy to lose sight of who we are as the royal family of Jesus Christ, even though we have this immense gift of grace inside. Through failure, disappointment or bad decisions we've made, negative results have a way of just sticking around in the back of our thoughts causing us to slowly lose sight of the design God has for our life. Traces of unhealthy thoughts toward "who we really are" begin to gradually show up through the relationships we choose, how we spend our time and what we allow in our life. For example, individuals will often settle for a mate, even though that person doesn't make them better or push them toward their dreams. Others will settle for friendships and social circles that speak death to them and never speak into their life. Why do they settle? This is because an unhealthy self-image has distorted their vision for life, causing them to lose sight of what they are really after. Is this you? God's grace has been lavished on you, and it is strong enough to overcome those negative ideas and self-destructive images. Your relationships, associations, habits, and actions should reflect that new and healthy inner image of yourself.

Your "inner" vision impacts your "outer" vision. That's why divine grace is needed to remind you of who you are to empower you to see yourself in a positive light even when you don't seem to be living up to your potential. Every time we miss the mark, divine grace makes up for it and covers us in God's favor. Grace is the mark of favor that pushes us to keep going even when we feel like giving up. Grace reinforces to us our heavenly kingship and honor in Christ our King. Grace is also the mark of royalty within us. It releases the splendor that is in us through Jesus' blood! Yes, the DNA of a King is flowing through you.

Deep within your inner man, there is a limitless king emerging through God's grace. The more you rely on grace and not your own ability you are shifting into your divine nature and waking up the king that's in you. Divine grace will empower you to lead a life of excellence simply by causing you to change your demeanor because the self-image of a king is becoming clearer to you. No matter what circumstances you may encounter or the situations you may find yourself faced with, you should always be conscious of your kingship; listening for the voice of your inner grace to release divine instruction to keep you on that path of righteousness. This is called being "strong" in the grace that is in you.

2 Timothy 2:1.

[You then, my son, be strong in the grace that is in Christ Jesus.]

Always remember grace is strength; it is supernatural power that flows from the presence of God. If you continually submit to grace, you submit to your hedge of protection and allow God's nature within you to be cultivated by faith emerging and growing season by season. Another simple definition of God's grace is: "God's divine enablement empowering you to succeed in all facets of life." The truth is you're royalty by blood and you have to become increasingly aware of that reality every day in order to see its impact take shape in your physical life.

The truth is you're royalty by blood and you have to become increasingly aware of that reality every day in order to see its impact take shape in your physical life.

One other thing you can do to increase in the grace within you is being intentional about stepping out

> **The truth is you're royalty by blood and you have to become increasingly aware of that reality every day in order to see its impact take shape in your physical life.**

on faith. When you take steps that are beyond your human potential, you tap into the abundance of God's inner grace allowing the king within you to spring forth and rule from the eternal unlimited place of Heaven. Acts of faith put a force on grace, because once you step beyond your natural ability you have died to yourself, and the new you inside must emerge to bring you into total victory. Remember the passage in Romans 5:

> [*We have gained access by faith into this grace in which we now stand.*]

So it is by "by faith" we access the unlimited benefits of Heaven's throne. The key to tapping into the law of grace is the activation of the law of faith. And that begins with your willingness to continually declare the Word and then take action on God's Word, regardless of the circumstances. By doing this you are leaving your earthly nature out of the equation and powering up grace. Simply put, you are allowing faith to put the responsibility on God's divine nature within you to make His Word come to pass. Live like a king! You deserve it! Jesus died to share His crown with you and His grace has given you access to every benefit of Heaven's throne, its richness, and its resources.

Growing in His grace also means we are learning to strategically draw from the wellspring of His presence within and use it to accelerate us on the path of destiny. God is saying to us, "Learn to use the power that I've put in you, and it will guarantee your victory." As you allow God's grace continually to increase within you, based on the winning power inside, you must begin to cultivate a winning attitude.

Though all things may not be good, we must be confident that our present conditions are working to produce a far greater outcome than what we are able to see.

> **Though all things may not be good, we must be confident that our present conditions are working to produce a far greater outcome than what we are able to see.**

A winning attitude begins with the belief system that no matter what challenges you may encounter, every obstacle is a set up to increase you. You have to believe this if you are going to function in the limitless reality of the Kingdom. Romans 8:30 puts it this way, *"And we know that all things work together for the good of those who love him."* Though all things may not be good, we must be confident that our present conditions are working to produce a far greater outcome than what we are able to see. You will not be able to experience all of the benefits of your present season, nor can you fully tap into kingship without being fully convinced that God is somehow working for your good. Adopt this idea and keep it at the front of your mind. I'm telling you, this type of confidence can create a positive shift for anyone despite the present level of difficulty they are facing.

This is the attitude of champions, learning to master a productive mindset despite the current challenges. They are much like the eagle who flies at his highest point in the midst of the storm by allowing the turbulence to push him to greater heights. Champions leverage the winds of adversity, turning their present storm into a launching pad for victory. They are always aware that "I'm endowed by God's throne of grace, and nothing can constrain me." Leveraging God's grace to develop a winning attitude is essential to creating turnaround in the midst of adversity.

A winning attitude is an essential element to living your life without limitations. Perhaps you are caught in the storm of failure or disappointment. Remain focused on the idea that God is committed to bringing you into the blessing He has already orchestrated out of your trial. This is another key to developing a winning mentality: realize that God is more committed to your breakthrough than you are!

In the 23rd Psalm, the writer mentions that God, the good shepherd, leads us beside still waters for HIS name's sake. This means God is so committed to making sure His name stays good, He will *not* let you fail. He is more committed to the vision than you are.

Now, no one can convince you of this but yourself. It may take time and some undoing of negative perspectives, but you must use God's principles to train the muscle of faith within you and began to believe that God is serious about your success.

You have to train your attitude and belief systems until you become unwavering about God's strategy and His burning desire to help you win at life. By doing this you'll create awareness and expectation that no matter how dark the season, breakthrough is always right around the corner. The best part is this: knowing that regardless of your failures, God in His omnipotence, somehow, can always use your setbacks to advance you. This is all a part of God's pre-designed plan to prosper and bless you. God's purpose for predestining your victory is to empower you to press the delete button on every discouraging thought and negative relationship in your life.

Champions understand that succeeding is never about avoiding failure, rather it's learning to use mistakes as spiritual fuel to power the engine of success. Understand that just because you have failed does not mean that you are a failure. Believing such negative ideas is toxic to your thought life and vision. There are no failures in Christ, only winners. God made it that that way.

Champions understand that succeeding is never about avoiding failure, rather it's learning to use mistakes as spiritual fuel to power the engine of success.

Success will not be measured by how many times you have failed, rather by your ability to bounce back from it. Disappointment will always be present in the face of failure. While a feeling of disappointment is a natural emotion when expectations aren't met, it isn't determinate on your situation. However, dwelling on your disappointment too long can cause an overwhelming feeling of hopelessness. Disappointment is the number one reason why people never try again. Disappointment when conceived gives birth to a failure mindset.

> **Champions understand that succeeding is never about avoiding failure, rather it's learning to use mistakes as spiritual fuel to power the engine of success.**

As a result many people enter into business and ministry endeavors with a constant fear of failure. Will I make it? How will I be received? These questions are irrelevant and become the focus of any individual's thought life when they stop looking at their purpose and start looking at the past.

To avoid this poison of disappointment keep looking at your purpose. Always remember your purpose is greater than your past. If you hold on to your purpose it will push you through the most discouraging times. No matter the disappointment, a true purpose is all you need to get back up and try again. Understand that your purpose is worth you trying again. The individuals that will be positively impacted by your dreams and visions are worth you trying again.

Don't concern yourself with failure, realize that failure is simply one of God's divine tools for teaching you how not to miss the next time. I've learned not to entertain thoughts of failure and that it's a natural stage up the mountain of achievement. There are two sides to every coin, which makes failures just as important as victories on the road of success. Remember that on the other side of failure is always a well worthy victory.

The Grace of Thanksgiving

As a result of God's grace within, you can stay focused on your vision while constantly taking some type of action toward seeing it come to pass. Even in turbulent times it's important to be intentional about making forward progress toward the manifestation of your dreams. I have found the more time I spend measuring my action toward vision the less time I have to worry about the contradictions around me.

It's also very important to develop an attitude of gratitude when trying to achieve any level of success. Remember to be thankful for every inch and step toward the materialization of your vision. Constant action should lead to a discipline of thanksgiving that you are one step closer to achievement today than you were yesterday. Even though at times, we would like to see more progress in the fulfillment of our dreams, we must dig deep, and tap into the grace that produces genuine praise and thanksgiving to God.

The more time you spend thanking God for positive progression the less time you have to worry about what isn't happening for you. Isaiah 60:1-5 reminds us that even though things on the outside may seem to be dark, moving slow or unfavorable, all we have to do is "look" around us and see that God's glory is covering us and there we will find uncontainable joy! What this really means is we have to realize through the eyes of the Spirit that we are a finished work, and by grace we are tapping into that complete plan. Every day we are one step closer to manifesting God's finished work within us.

I remember when I launched my leadership/coaching business, "Blueprint Global Leadership Training". I wanted to begin teaching leadership and life enrichment seminars, workshops, and academies all over the country. The idea of Blueprint Training was that in every person God has invested His personal blueprint that can teach us to lead our most compelling life. By tapping into that blueprint, any person can learn to dominate, become a better leader and increase their overall quality of life. The only problem was I didn't have any open doors, physically, at the time.

There was absolutely no one aware of what I was doing and I didn't even have the credentials that most churches, businesses and other organizations look for when outsourcing leadership training. Once, I sat down with one of my mentors, someone whom I respected highly and was a corporate executive one of America's largest fortune 100 companies. I'll never forget her response when I told her about my vision for Blueprint Training. She told me that I couldn't do it because I lacked the credibility most organizations and corporations look for when it comes to leadership training. My mouth almost dropped to my lap. I was astonished that I was hearing this from my mentor. Now, since I understood that "I can't" is not a Kingdom philosophy, I knew her words were not my responsibility to take on; they were reflections of her own insecurities. This is the situation with most people who tell you what you cannot do.

When people say "you can't" do something you are passionately pursuing, understand what they really mean is "I can't" or "I would be afraid to try something like that." Dreamers always expose the insecurities of limited thinkers around them. Absolutely, under no circumstance, should you listen to or internalize others' insecurities as your own.

Dreamers always expose the insecurities of limited thinkers around them.

> **Dreamers always expose the insecurities of limited thinkers around them.**

As faith would have it, I didn't allow her words to be the last governing authority over my vision. I began to speak and decree a different outcome: that since I was in the Kingdom, I had the credentials of Jesus, the greatest leadership coach ever, and through empowering grace, His leadership potential (power) was in me. As God divinely and strategically used His Word to strengthen my heart, His divine reality opened up to me even more. Every day I would work to sharpen my teaching curriculums and learning strategies.

I would spend countless hours thinking of innovative coaching techniques and leadership strategies to distinguish "Blueprint" from the other organizations in the leadership market. Soon God adjusted my vision and overall perception of what He was after through my training enterprise. He began to lead me to mentors and other successful entrepreneurs who could help develop my understanding and overall performance as a coach and leader. Eventually Blueprint Global Leadership Training became "Blueprint Training International" and alongside a strong and effective leadership initiative, I was able to add a lucrative personal coaching business and life enrichment program to the Blueprint umbrella.

Of course it didn't happen overnight. I started out teaching leadership and doing training seminars for free! Although it was challenging at times I knew I was sowing into the future of a successful enterprise. Eventually the word got out more and more about Blueprint and I began to receive invitations and paid contracts to train, teach and coach locally, regionally, nationally, and now internationally. The breakthrough was not in the invitations; it lied in the fact that I was prepared, because I was confident in my gift through Christ and I never stopped making progress toward my vision. I was often tempted to soak in negative thinking about the fact that I was not getting any invites to speak or that I wasn't gaining any clients to personally coach. I was faced with the choice to view my situation as unproductive and purposeless or I could see it as an open door for Heaven's supernatural laws to transact to me exactly what I had been standing in faith for.

Part of creating real turnaround has to do with us being able to recognize divine doors or seasons of opportunity regardless of how they may appear to the natural eye. God had revealed to me that I should not see myself as a person without a full itinerary; rather I should view myself as a fully credentialed leadership expert and trainer with extra time and opportunity to invest more creativity and planning into my curriculums and programs. Soon, I realized that I possessed superior capabilities compared to other leadership and coaching businesses, because of the time, innovation, and cutting edge sciences that differentiated Blueprint.

See, you have to be able to adjust your spiritual lens and realize that every situation is an opportunity to birth something new and creative in you. This is also what is called having a "kingdom mindset." It's when, by tapping into God's laws by faith, we trigger something so powerful in our own hearts that the idea and perspective of the King becomes our perspective also. We then have no choice but to view the situation through His perspective of grace and no longer through our own. So be thankful, whether one verse to a song for an aspiring singer or one more idea toward the vision for building an organization. Thank God for every step that brings you closer to your vision and He will honor you with good success.

The Grace to Change

Sometimes people can be so concerned with the 'why' of what they are facing they never learn the 'what' and its purpose. As blurry as things may appear at times, God is not trying to hide the purpose of our season from us. It is not some mystery that one has to discover through deep religious activity. It's simply a matter of stepping back and assessing the situation with patience until we began to understand the change that is taking place in our lives. Change has to come in order for growth to take place, yet people are fearful when change shows its face.

A healthy perspective of change is definitely needed if you are going to successfully transition into a new season. Some changes are much more complex, and may take more focus and concentration to understand. Nevertheless I have found that the better we are able to grasp and articulate the change we are experiencing, the better we are able to benefit from it. Some people never fully break through because there is no one in their life to help them grasp the basis of what is taking place.

When this happens, what God has intended for growth can become a place of death. The determinate factor is the understanding you have of the change, its purpose, and the direction God is trying to push you into. Consequently, without this knowledge you will end up always feeling like you are on the verge of something happening, but it seems to never quite take form. These are usually individuals who could not effectively define the season of change they were in and the purpose God was after through their change. This is called the process of "transition."

There can be no real change if a proper transitioning doesn't take place. During transition, things can seem to become confusing and chaotic. However, I have found that what we often view as chaos may be called and seen as transition. The pressure of change never just pushes us; it always pushes us into some direction. The persecution of the church pushed Philip into Samaria, but it was really God pushing him into destiny. To fully transition from one stage to the next, be prayerful to God about the direction He is pushing you toward.

Most seasons of change and transitioning start with a prophetic word given to someone. The prophetic word is very important to launching real change in someone's life. Problems happen in the church when they fail to realize that the prophetic word is prophetic law; another subsystem of the Kingdom intended to help shift the members of Christ's body into His divinely appointed direction. It's another divine grace, which we can strategically use to open new doors around us.

What I am trying to say is, don't get stuck at a word, vision, or dream. Learn how to use that word to create a positive shift by allowing the pressure of the change it brings to propel you into a greater understanding of what God wants for you. If you can grasp God's heart for your life through every season of change, you will always transition fully, continuously gravitating towards God's best for your life.

The Grace to Accelerate

As I mentioned earlier, Kingdom living is experiencing God's best in your everyday life. The principle of understanding times and seasons makes it important for us to closely examine our relationships and common surroundings in times of intense change. Bad advice or negative influence from a bad relationship can cause a cycle of emotional rollercoasters as you try to decipher between what is good for you and what is best. For this reason I encourage you to be intentional with fervency in your prayers in the area of discernment concerning your relationships.

Often times who we allow in our "inner circle" can make the difference in our clarity when determining what direction God's wants us to take. As you pray this, you can be sure that you will begin to see the relationships around you shift. So, when this shift begins to happen get excited, because relationships are always signs that point us to our new season. In other words, when the people around you begin to change that is one of God's ways of letting you know your season is changing.

When the people around you begin to change that is one of God's ways of letting you know your season is changing.

I always remind people that the confidence to change relationships lies in the understanding that change

When the people around you begin to change that is one of God's ways of letting you know your season is changing.

is never about what or who you're letting go, but it's always about the new God wants you to embrace. That "new" is always His best and will join you to His perfect plan every time you trust God and follow the new direction He is pushing you in.

The moment we make the decision to choose God's best for us rather than what is good for us, we accelerate the path to blessings. One of the greatest challenges lies not in deciding between what is good and what is bad for us. The issue for most people is when they are faced with the dilemma of deciding what is good for them and what is God's best for them. I have often found that man will tell us what's good for us, but God will speak to us based on what is best.

That is why it's important to receive the counsel of others, but only in constituency of the counsel of God. Both sound beneficial, accept what is good doesn't necessarily guarantee a change of seasons. You have to remember that the strength of decision-making lies in its ability to end and begin new seasons for you. This means deciding to choose God's best can position you into a place of constant acceleration. Acceleration means you are continually experiencing new seasons and blessings along with new breakthrough in your life. It means you're thriving. In acceleration you have tapped into God's law of increase, which He established man with upon giving him His government in Eden. (Genesis1:28).

I found that the law of increase isn't about "how much." Rather, increase deals with how consistently and how fast we receive something. Did you know God wants to get what you have prayed for to you as fast as possible? That's why He gave us instant access to His Blessing by empowering us with His grace on the inside of us. That's immediate access. For this reason God advises us, not with what is good for us, but with what is best for us.

Though God's best isn't always what's most comfortable you can be sure that obedience to what He says will always bring what we need in efficient timing. So we have to get over wanting only what's good for us and begin seeking God's best. When we only choose what is good for us, it can create comfort. However, the good we may feel at the time can cause comfort and may become our greatest opposition to promotion and good success.

One of the ways to do this is to manage closely who we get advice from, especially in tough times. It's imperative that we silence the voices around us as we try to grasp the heart of the changes that we are experiencing. As the external voices decrease, God's internal voice will increase. This will teach us what's best and how to make decisions that will fully transition us into the next season of life with blessing and acceleration.

Keys to Creating a Turnaround

1. **Develop a winning attitude.**
   God is committed to His good name.

   - Commit to unleashing the champion in you by tapping into God's empowering grace.
   - Acknowledge the grace within you.
   - Become convinced, "I will always win."
   - Remain encouraged that: "no matter what God is working for my good and everything is a set up for my victory."
   - God is more committed to seeing the vision come to pass than you are.

2. **Break the spirit of failure.**
   Don't look at your past, look at your purpose.

   - Champions understand that winning is about leveraging failure to fuel the engine of success.
   - Just because you have failed doesn't make you a failure.

- Your purpose is always greater than your past and is reason to try again.
- Failure is a natural step up the mountain of success.

3. **Measure Your Progress with Praise.**

   Thank God for every inch and step toward the manifestation of your dreams.

   - Change how you view the circumstance by recognizing fresh opportunity for growth and creativity.
   - No matter the seasons, always be intentional about making some forward progress toward seeing your vision come to pass.
   - The more time you spend making progress in your vision the less time you have to concentrate on what isn't happening.

4. **Define the season.**

   Change is essential to growth.

   - Take time to examine and articulate the change taking place.
   - An understanding of change is needed to fully transition into a new season.
   - Pray for discernment in relationships in time of intense change.
   - New relationships mark new seasons.

5. **Good vs. God's Best**

   Man says what's good. God says what is best.

   - Choosing God's best will accelerate the path to His blessings.
   - Constant acceleration is the mark of good decision-making.
   - Bad relationships can frustrate change.
   - Only choosing what's good can cause comfort, which is the #1 enemy to achievement.

8

The Hunger in Vision: Kingdom Pursuit

"Hunger is the handmaid of Genius." — Mark Twain,
American humorist, writer and lecturer

Hunger Drive

According to Merriam Webster, hunger is the discomfort, weakness or pain caused by a prolonged lack of food. When most people think of hunger they think of their physical body. But since we know that lack and hunger aren't elements of the Blessing, how can we apply this definition to our spiritual nourishment, lives, and souls? How can we apply this to our desire to encounter a Kingdom without limits?

With all the distractions of the world giving our spirits a steady diet of junk food is it possible to still hunger for God's Word and His Kingdom? How can that hunger lead us to better revelation, insight and skill for applying His Word and reshaping our world to better reflect Him?

How do we nurture our new spiritual diet so that it empowers our desire for good spiritual food? Food that has been blessed and has His Blessing. Spiritual food that completes us and connects us to His power and gives us access to His authority. Food that doesn't leave us feeling empty and sick at the table. Food that heals and is not filled with fat and sugar.

Just like our physical body needs to be nourished, our spiritual being has to be cultivated in order to manifest the design God has placed in us to live out of. What many have failed to truly pay attention to is the fact that just like our physical bodies, our spiritual diets are lacking.

Our "hunger" makes us reach for something that will fulfill us, but without knowledge and guidance what are we truly digesting? Our "hunger" to fulfill our spirits causes us to reach and pull and that action of reaching and pulling produces a product.

That is why it is so necessary to train our hunger and to develop our spiritual desires so that when we are pulling, we are pulling to reach the Lord and not pulling on something that is tearing us away from Him.

Let's look at the word "heaven." In the word heaven is the word heave. Heave means to raise or lift, especially with great force or effort. In order to access heaven's reality, there has to be effort, not just effort but great effort. There has to be that heaving, that pulling and pushing; that rising and swelling.

That swelling comes from our passion and desire for the Kingdom, which is really God's heart. If our passion is distracted or nullified do you believe it will idle? NO! It will find another source to fill up on. We can call this junk food. Spiritually you will find something else to satiate your passion and hunger that you should have had for God and His Kingdom, and that hunger will pull you into a world that feeds your craving.

This is our problem today; not that we are not being fed but that we are feeding on the wrong things. Consequently, the Word of God is not able to properly nourish us because we have not hungered after its richness. This causes us to lack the divine presence of His reality we desire to experience in our everyday life.

Hunger Power

Effort is not labor, nor is it sweating. It is simply constant practice of the Word generating an unstoppable flow of God's unlimited power. It's having a spiritual stubbornness that at all costs you are going to stand on the laws of God until they see you through. It is also continuous applied force to what we know is true and actually works.

One of the reasons people fail to experience real Kingdom living is that they try aligning with it and walking in some of its principles for a little while, but if they don't see results fast enough they give up. Another reason is if the right (or wrong) storm hits, they abort God's way and go back to what is familiar, the earth cursed mentality where fear, worry, and labor govern. This is why a healthy spiritual drive is necessary in your pursuit of the Kingdom. Remember that most of us have spent our lives thinking and operating in a system that is contrary to God's way of doing things. Therefore, we need to be patient when renewing our minds and making the transition to the blessed life.

Your patience, as God is gradually reshaping your world with His Word, will determine the overall results you get and the level of breakthrough and manifestation you see. If real God-hunger isn't present, you'll give up in the face of adversity and feel as though God's law isn't working and that you are wasting your time.

When there is a true spiritual hunger, quitting is never an option. Even in the face of what would normally seem impossible, hunger will cause you to rise and empower you to face your fears. It will give you the will power to act in spite of all your insecurities. True hunger says *"I never lose,"* and knows that in every battle victory is waiting to be obtained. Jesus never lost a battle, fight with temptation, or struggle of any kind. He did have battles to overcome and He was tempted, but He was always victorious. Why? Because of the drive that was in Him, His hunger to see God's Kingdom manifested in the earth.

His attitude was: "God's glory has to be revealed through my life." He knew that beyond all fleshly limits there was always a power within Him to overcome all odds. Now, I understand that we as human beings living in imperfect flesh will constantly experience our share of failures. However, I'm convinced that it is not a reason to accept the struggle and lay down in it. You are a possessor of the redeeming power that raised Jesus from the dead. Thus, He gave the same overcoming power and spirit to all of us who are a part of His royal family. John 14:27:

> *[In this world you will have trouble, but do not be afraid for I have overcome this world.]* Your "spiritual drive" is your "hunger" and that same drive pushes us to keep moving forward even in what may seem like the worst of times.

Quitting isn't in your spiritual DNA; winning is. And your expectation should rise from your hunger to be a living, breathing testimony of the limitless power of the Kingdom.

How Hunger Unlocks the Blessing.

As I said earlier, you must have patience when tapping into the Blessing of God's Kingdom. First, be confident in what you have read in the Word. Let go of your commitment to emotion, fear and pressure. Put your foot down and make the commitment to whole-heartedly believe, trust, and act only on the Word. The reason you must have patience when breaking into the Blessing is not because God needs time to do anything. Again, as I said before, everything God is going to do He's done it through His Kingdom. That's why He's been resting since Genesis. We must have patience because *we* have spent so much time in a diametrically opposed system and way of thinking that we have to readapt to His way of life. Through constant repetition of Word application we are cultivating and grooming our hearts to expect His Kingdom reality. We need time to renew our minds, spirits, and realign our thought order with the alignment and structure of God's heart. Depending on how deep your religious roots run and how long you've been thinking a certain way, the process of renewal can take more or less time varying from person to person.

Nevertheless, you can set your hearts to believe that the Word always works! Living by faith always works! The Kingdom is real and if you stay with God's mindset and His way of doing things you are on your way to victory and bearing a fruitful harvest that you will be able to feed from for the rest of your life. This is where your spiritual hunger comes in. Training yourself to have a healthy appetite for truth and revelation can make the difference when it comes to "crossing over" to the "blessed life."

In Joshua 1, Joshua, the leader of Israel, is commanded by the Lord to instruct the people to "get ready" to cross over the Jordan Sea to possess the promise of the Blessing—the land He swore to their forefathers (Abraham, Isaac, and Jacob) to give them. The expression "get ready" or "prepare yourselves" did not mean to pack luggage and clothes. It is an expression that literally means: "go through and decide what you need most for the trip because everything you possess cannot come along with you" (the Jordan Sea was a long walk, about 40 days to cross). The children of Israel could only bring the essentials with them, which makes sense because they were about to cross through a sea and they had to travel light. Also, God did not want them bringing resources from the previous land because they were walking into a place of provision, where everything had already been supplied. This generation of followers was not like the previous generation. They did not argue with Joshua or complain, they simply replied, "Whatever you say we'll do it." Their hunger to see God's promise fulfilled created a submissive and obedient heart within them. Though they could not physically see what was on the other side, their faith had sparked such a hunger in them that taking action on God's promise was inevitable.

After making the necessary adjustments and changes, they were ready. The most amazing part: they were given only 3 days to do so! When God moves, it's going to be fast! You see, you have to be ready to move with God and make the necessary changes if you are going to shift into Heaven's reality. You cannot bring your previous sustenance and your way of thinking from your previous life into the land of the promise.

Many people want to stay the same, think the same, and hang onto old relationships and still expect to walk in the fullness of God's supernatural reality. You have to be hungry enough to make the necessary adjustments and cut off all unnecessary baggage. This is a hard truth for people to swallow so they remain the same and never experience life the way God intended.

The Kingdom is not for spiritual slouches or carnal individuals. It is for disciplined people, hungry-hearted believers who have decided that Heaven's reality is going to become their reality no matter the cost. So then it becomes imperative that as you as transition from one reality to the next you are constantly training your ears to new truth, faith teaching and Kingdom philosophy. **Your time is one of your most valuable resources, and you can't afford to invest in areas that don't yield a positive return.**

Be sure to measure your time wisely, and not invest it in areas that leave you spiritually bankrupt. Your time is one of your most valuable resources, and you can't afford to invest in areas that don't yield a positive return. As you do this, the results will gradually begin to show up and the fruit of your faith will only incite greater hunger to keep pressing forward. That pressing is genuine passion to see God's plan fulfilled in your life. Paul, the apostle, was driven by the same hunger. Despite the many struggles and obstacles that he faced in his life and ministry, he was just as hungry to possess Heaven's promises as he was when he began. Look at Philippians 3:14

> *[I press on to reach the end of the race and receive the heavenly prize for which God, through Christ Jesus, is calling us.]*

God has called you to experience victory in the earth to obtain a prize that only Heaven can reward.

A Kingdom Revolution

As you become more and more immersed in a Kingdom ideology, a heavenly revolution should resonate within your heart. The impractical will become practical and the impossible will simply become a matter of faith and the operation of God's supernatural law. You'll begin to crave God's heart and God's law after seeing God's spiritual power manifested not only in your life, but in the lives of those you meet. What remains then, is a pure hunger to continue to see God's glory and nature manifested in your life.

True Kingdom hunger is never about us, because when we access the Kingdom we arrive at God's original intention for man and creation. This means our real hunger is emerging from a deep passion within to see God's original vision for mankind fulfilled. We become driven by the genuine desire to see His glory cover the earth as He set out to do when He established the Garden of Eden. Since we are His body, we know this can only be done through us.

When God sees this attitude He is pleased. He gets excited along with us and wants nothing more than to fill you with the abundant riches of His blessing all the more. Why? Because you are now both operating out of the same mind, same heart, and same vision. You will have allowed His Kingdom to subdue your heart and revolutionize your reality. You see, real God-Hunger will always lead you to alignment with God's purpose. As a result the flow of blessing is endless and uncontained. As the condition of your heart will have aligned with God's true purpose and desire of His heart, obtaining Heaven will have never been easier. And you'll soon see that He is going to give you greater access to greater resources to accomplish His will in the earth.

Vision Hunger

A key to really unleashing abundance in your life is seeking God's vision in whatever you do. Many times, pastors and leaders in the ministry become so caught up with *their* vision they forget to really search and seek the heart of the Holy Spirit as to what His original concept or idea for that particular project was. On the road to accomplishing vision it's always good to revisit our source, the King, and His intention for what we are doing. When we do this, we constantly remind ourselves that it isn't our project, it's God's.

Now, if you forget this you'll become stressed out during the process of manifesting your vision, and this should not be. Remember that the Blessing takes the sorrow out of living. Sorrow includes labor, toil, sweat, and all forms of stress; every trait of the cursed world system. You must remember that as earthly representatives we are on diplomatic assignment, which means we are only managing God's affairs, not ours, in the earth. We are His body, not our own. We died to ours and the life we now live is hidden in Christ (Colossians 3:3-4). So, in essence, you don't have problems. You don't have to come up with solutions, Jesus does. That's why He is the head. Simply tap into your "Head" who is your source (Christ) and make His principles work for you.

When we think this way, focusing our thoughts and intention on what the King wants out of every work we put our hands to, the project is no longer ours alone, but it also belongs to God. This is where a lot of ministries get in trouble. However, if you can remember to apply this principle of faith and hunger, you will never lack or want in anything you endeavor to do. This is because whatever belongs to the King He is responsible for taking care of, making provision for, and funding. God hasn't asked us to pay for anything He's called us to do, nor has He ever asked man to make provision for something He wanted us to accomplish.

Here is something else that may surprise you; God really hasn't asked us to start anything nor has He asked us to finish it. I know that may sound a little odd, but think about this for a moment: Jesus already told you *"It's finished"* (John 19:30). If that pertained to your salvation don't you think it also includes your vision?

As far as starting something, the Bible already let you know that *"He who began a good work in you is also faithful to complete it."* (Philippians 1:16). So what has God really asked of you? The answer is simple; our assignment as foreign agents in the earth is to manage the processes and transactions of Jesus, our King. He has only asked us to be administrators and stewards over what He has already done. Steward His money, His church, and His people. This was Adam's assignment in Eden, and it's still our assignment now. Adam was only given rule over what God had already established.

When we lack true hunger for God's purpose in our vision, we cause confusion, unnecessary pressure, and unwanted burden. That's not the Blessing, it's sorrow, and it comes from the curse. Jesus didn't die for you to have burdens in order to accomplish your dream. He came to give you rest, take up your burden and exchange it with His, which is easy and light in weight (Matthew 28:11).

Bringing the vision to pass shouldn't be grievous. This only happens when people lose focus of God's main idea and purpose for the vision and who is really in charge of making it come to pass. I certainly don't want you to misunderstand my purpose in saying all of this. There is nothing wrong with having vision, creating and building. There is a great responsibility on the believer of taking that vision to the next level. However, you must remember you are the body and Christ is the Head, which means your vision should flow from the top down, and then you should develop your vision around what God has already shown you.

Hunger after His insights, be pursuant of God's heart in the matter and ask Him questions daily concerning His plan for your vision. You'll soon find that even though God is King, He is still waiting for us to persistently seek His insight and invite Him into our plans.

How Vision Increases Hunger

As you are developing a strong spiritual hunger, another important key to releasing the Blessing is learning how to maintain that hunger. Daily our spiritual hunger experiences all kinds of attacks. How do you stay excited about the Kingdom along with the vision God has given you? With so many obstacles and distractions constantly being thrown at us and trying to take our passion for living, how do we stay motivated about God's plan for our lives?

We must remain conscious of *"hunger attacks."* However, the answer to staying motivated does not lie in creating a strategy to protect our hunger; it lies in the power of maintaining vision. If you want to maintain hunger and drive, you have to maintain vision. You see, the more you are able to see, the more you will hunger after in life. No matter how many obstacles a person faces in their pursuit of success, if they can continue to produce vision, their hunger will continue to increase.

The answer to staying motivated does not lie in creating a strategy to protect our hunger; it lies in the power of maintaining vision.

For example, have you ever noticed how you can be watching a commercial or advertisement of your favorite restaurant and begin to get hungry? We

> The answer to staying motivated does not lie in creating a strategy to protect our hunger; it lies in the power of maintaining vision.

all have. Sometimes you don't even have to be thinking about food, but when that commercial begins to play, your eyes get big, and your saliva glands begin to salivate based on what the eye gates see. Next thing we know, that picture stays in the back of our minds floating around and most likely the next time we're hungry that's the place we'll go to eat. You see, what we see will always perpetuate what we hunger after.

Even if you are a successful person in business, ministry, or any other endeavor, your ability to produce new vision will be the key to never burning out. I like to say it this way: "Vision is the vitality of Christian living."

Vision is the source of hunger. You cannot stop looking at your vision. You will remain hungry as long as you have something to look at. Many times people have become exasperated with their dreams and lost hope for seeing them come to pass. What happened? They stopped looking at the vision. They got distracted from their vision, and the circumstances around them began to overwhelm their faith.

I know it is often said: "faith is believing without seeing." The actual truth is that faith believes as a result of seeing. Faith becomes our eyes in the spirit that allows us to see what God has promised us. That's why faith comes by hearing, because the hearing of God's Word and His promises create a mental image for us to look at. When God speaks to us it is to create a picture in our minds. If we allow that image to become distorted, our hope will quickly begin to fade.

The attacks toward our dreams are what I call *"vision distracters."* One of the most important parts of living free from limitations is your ability maintain your vision. Without it you don't have much to look forward to in your life. While I have heard much reasoning that the enemy is after so many different things in our lives, I am most convinced he is after our vision. Look at 1 Peter 5:8:

> *[Your enemy, the Devil, is like a roaring lion look for whom he may destroy.]*

Now look at Proverbs 23:18:

> *[Where there is no vision people are destroyed.]*

As we examine both passages we see that destruction is the main idea. What you see though, in the second passage, is that not having a vision is the weapon that is used to create that destruction. Lack of vision is a powerful tool against Christians designed to discourage our hope for living. Maintaining your vision can be a challenge, and to be successful against that challenge we must be able to recognize "vision distracters" when they come.

Signs of Distraction

I could tell you how much I continually focus on my vision, but the truth is that I too, know what it's like to become derailed from purpose. Many times in my life I can always tell when I have lost my focal point, because things around me become extremely disorderly and frustrating. Please don't misunderstand. I do believe that no matter what season of life we are in we will experience some sort of challenge. However, when things become so frustrating to the point that you are becoming burned out it's usually because you have lost sight of your vision. It is very possible for something that God intended for the purpose of building you up to end up burning you out. Many of us have experienced this. Proverbs 13:12 tells us *"Hope deferred makes the heart sick."* God doesn't want you to become burned out with your vision, but without an understanding of how vision works and the keys to maintaining it, frustration is always sure to come.

Recently in one of my coaching sessions, I spent some time with a client who had moved to a new city. They were in need of help regaining vision and purpose for their life. They had become extremely frustrated on the job, frustrated with their church and frustrated in their relationships. One of the concepts I teach in personal coaching is that "purpose is the enemy of frustration." You see, passion is designed to fuel purpose. If you have a strong grasp of a clear purpose for anything and an understanding of what that purpose is, it will be hard for anyone or anything to frustrate or distract you.

So, step-by-step we began to examine the previous year, certain occurrences and recent stages in their life. What we realized was that they had totally become disconnected from their vision, and as a result they had aborted their purpose for moving to that new city in the first place! Once we were able locate to their *vision distracters*, and recapture their vision and goals, the frustration was alleviated!

There is nothing wrong with pausing in life to examine where we've come from, where we presently stand and where we are going. It's easy to start on a certain path in a certain direction and with one distraction after another we sometimes end up opposite to the direction we were originally headed. We all have to take a moment in life to step back and assess things.

Periodically we should all do what I call taking a "spiritual fiscal report." At the end of every fiscal year, businesses undergo a *fiscal analysis*—an annual report to recap losses and profits, set budgets and decide based on the previous year what necessary adjustments need to be made in order to continue in a healthy pursuit of the mission and vision of their company. Sometimes certain projects are salvageable and other times they have to do what is called "cut their losses." Basically, they revisit their goals and create an action strategy to attain them based on what they have left. You see, it's pointless to waste time in life mourning over what you've lost, but you can always create a plan to move forward with what you've got left. You have God's abundant grace within you. That means somewhere inside there is still a plan to succeed and it's waiting to be tapped into.

Are you feeling burned out in life or in your vision? Maybe it's time to take a "spiritual fiscal analysis". Go back and examine the last year or two, or maybe even the last 3-5 years. At what point did you lose sight of your vision? Was it a past experience of failure and deep disappointment that paralyzed your dream? Was it in a past relationship that didn't work out? Did you allow family issues or other complications to cause you to put the vision down for a while? Maybe it's time to *cut your losses.* Revisit God's purpose and original intent for giving you that vision and take time to examine some of the distractions you failed to cut out. Once you've realized them, make the adjustments and let go of the past. Ask God to be the source of your vision, to give you a bigger and better picture to focus on and a strategy to pursue it. You'll notice your hunger will begin to emerge once again and a new passion for life will began to empower your spiritual and personal drive. Whatever your vision is, remember that God still has a plan for it, and His promise of that vision is still waiting to come to pass!

Vision Power

Let's look at some vision principles that can help you maintain and increase your vision as well as power your hunger for God, life, and success.

1. God is faithful to the vision: (Jeremiah 1:12)

[You have seen correctly, for I am watching to see that my word is fulfilled.]

The Law of vision: If God shows it to you, then it already exists for you in the spirit. A vision is a snapshot that reflects the image of an already existent thing. God will never show a picture of something that isn't already there.

2. The Law of possession: If you are able to see or envision it, then you have already taken possession of it. (Genesis 13:15)

   [I am giving all this land, as far as you can see, to you and your descendants as a permanent possession.]

3. Enlarge your vision, enlarge your destiny: Every time your vision increases your destiny changes. As your vision increases you see more into the limitless possibilities of Heaven's reality. The more you see, the more God must give you. That's the law of possession. As much as you can *see* God will give you.

4. The vision comes with provision attached: If God gives you a vision then He has already set in place every provision for anything you'll need to accomplish it.

5. Your vision should be developed based on what God's purpose and intent for that vision are: Don't lose sight of God's heart for your vision, ask Him questions and continually seek His input.

6. Tunnel "vision" concept: Being consumed with your vision is essential to its manifestation. "There is no great genius without a mixture of madness." — Aristotle. For the joy set before Jesus He endured the cross. He was willing to give up everything to see God's purpose fulfilled through His vision. Are you?

7. Vision is law, not emotion: Emotion doesn't influence vision; it only makes the vision blurry and leads to a weary and sick heart. Remember God is a spiritual King and emotions do not move Him; only law does. Tapping into vision provokes God's supernatural power in your life.

8. A greater God-vision will increase your inner vision: The greater your inner vision, the larger your outer vision. Hunger intensifies as God reveals greater dimensions of Himself. Enlarge your vision by gaining a greater revelation of God and His Kingdom.

9. The grasshopper complex: Self-development increases inner vision. How you see yourself will determine how big your vision is and whether or not you lay hold of it. (Numbers 13:33) ["*We saw the giants and we seemed like grasshoppers in their sight.*"] Israel missed their appointed time of the Blessing because they didn't have a good inner vision to see beyond their own limitations. You must develop your self-image.

5 Keys that Will Create Clarity

There are 3 levels to vision: hearing, sight and clarity. All three combine to bring the entire picture of your vision into full manifestation. Let's look at Mark 8:22-26:

> *[They came to Bethsaida, and some people brought a blind man and begged Jesus to touch him. He took the blind man by the hand and led him outside the village. When he had spit on the man's eyes and put his hands on him, Jesus asked, "Do you see anything?" He looked up and said, "I see people; they look like trees walking around." Once more Jesus put his hands on the man's eyes. Then his eyes were opened, his sight was restored, and*

he saw everything clearly. Jesus sent him home, saying, "Don't even go into the village."]

Hearing: First the man heard about Jesus coming and listened to Him minister about him receiving his sight as it was a part of God's divine plan (John 9:6).

Sight: Next Jesus spit on some dirt and rubbed it in his eyes and was asked if he could *see* anything. His reply was "yes" but his new vision was still blurry and men appeared to him as trees.

Clarity: A second time Jesus touched his eyes and the Bible says: "He saw everything *clearly.*"

Hearing God is essential to seeing His plan for you. In order to operate in the law of vision, a healthy hunger to hear and receive revelation from God is absolutely imperative. From there, God will expand His vision within you and began to help you apply His principles to add clarity to that vision and your personal life.

Now let's look at these 5 principles to creating better clarity:

1. The Yes factor: The first step to adding clarity to your vision is telling God "yes." Yes, however is more than a word. *Yes* says: "God we can do this!" There must be an agreement in your heart and a belief that God is not only able to bring it to pass, but that you have the grace to see it through. *Yes* also means you have weighed the costs and understand some of the commitment it will take to bring the vision to pass. If you haven't thought about this, then saying yes won't be worth your time. There are plenty of individuals who have told God yes with no real intention of taking action on His promise. On the other hand, there are people who have failed to see promise after promise come to pass simply because they

never told God, "Yes, I agree that you are able to do this." It takes a perfect balance of both sides; a *yes* of true agreement, and a committed heart to stay with that promise and see it through until the end. Once you say yes and agree then you are ready to see further into the plan God has for you. From here the vision enlarges and becomes clearer. Divine strategy is laid out and a clear function of how to proceed is gradually revealed.

2. Grasp the concept and purpose of your vision God has shown you through prayer and listening to the wisdom of God's voice. Write down that purpose and concept and commit to periodically revisiting it through your process. You may find that as your vision increases, part of the vision may also and your plan of attack may need to as well.

3. Get around successful individuals who are prospering in the area or field you are pursuing. Ask questions. Learn about common obstacles they faced and how you can avoid some of those pitfalls. Watch them closely and put a demand on their time so that you can draw from their experience. You shouldn't pursue anything without getting connected with at least one other person who has succeeded in that area and can give positive feedback and helpful insight.

4. Expect a learning curve. Whenever you set out to do something there is always a learning curve involved. For example, when you move to a new city you have to learn the culture and adapt to the new lifestyle. This takes time and patience until some familiarity begins to kick in and soon the transition begins to smoothen out as you complete your adjustment. Similarly, when you are attempting to pursue a new vision, there may be some learning curves ahead. Expect them. Take the time to understand the mechanics of what you're pursuing and learn to develop a level of mastery in it as well. This will make your journey a lot smoother and will also

help you to keep focus on the vision during those challenging times. During that learning curve stage there will be some adverse times, and by learning some of the things to expect, you will be equipped with the confidence needed to stick with the plan so that you will not abort the vision in the storm.

5. Create an action strategy with specifics such as a projected launch date. Your detailed plan of action will hold you accountable and give better tracking power when it comes to measuring progress. Not only that, but by breaking your strategy down into simple daily tasks, you'll find the vision will not seem so overwhelming. Those daily victories will create confidence and help you to gradually build momentum in the right direction to accomplish your dream.

Hunger Pursuit: The Nicodemus Complex

A genuine hunger and desire after God's Kingdom requires the right angle of pursuit. The right angle of pursuit is governing your heart with the Word and allowing it to point you in the direction of God. This means that wildly and aimlessly chasing after God with all types of religious activity will never get His attention, nor will it create the breakthrough you desire to see.

God is a King. He is systematic and operates by law. No matter how much He loves you He isn't going to break His law for you. He is a God of order and even submits Himself to His own law and arrangement (Psalm 138:2). This means you must cultivate a Kingdom diet that hungers after the Word and the supreme laws of God, because without it, Heaven isn't going to be able to influence your life very much. Hunger is God's program for success. And His Word is the capsule through which all of His abundant resources are released. However, when it comes to Kingdom pursuit your approach must be correct. Although this is not widely taught in the church, it is the most critical part to living and operating in the Kingdom life. Jesus, as the Head, requires full alignment with His thoughts in order for His system to completely impact your life.

If you don't understand His modus of thinking or His approach to life you'll always be out of alignment with Him, hindering your progress and manifestation. A lot of believers have a genuine hunger to encounter God, but their approach to Him is so misaligned He cannot help them the way He desires to. A pure heart and intent are great, but they aren't what manifest God's presence. Alignment with His spiritual law does.

Therefore our hunger must be adjusted from everything that takes our focus off of the principles of God to focusing on proper alignment with His system and Kingdom truths. This includes not begging when we pray, or constantly repeating ourselves to God about the same thing and breaking the tendency to rely on anyone else to bring us out other than God. None of these are in alignment with a correct pursuit of God's Kingdom. If we don't catch this principle we cannot 'see' His precious government, and if we can't see it we cannot possess it, and without possession of it we will not be able to live in it. A good example of wrong Kingdom pursuit is found in what I call the "Nicodemus" principle: John 3:1-8

[Now there was a Pharisee, a man named Nicodemus who was a member of the Jewish ruling council. He came to Jesus at night and said, "Rabbi, we know that you are a teacher who has come from God. For no one could perform the signs you are doing if God were not with him." Jesus replied, "Very truly I tell you, no one can see the kingdom of God unless they are born again." "How can someone be born when they are old?" Nicodemus asked. "Surely they cannot enter a second time into their mother's womb to be born!" Jesus answered, "Very truly I tell you, no one can enter the kingdom of God unless they are born of water and the Spirit. Flesh gives birth to flesh, but the Spirit-man gives birth to spirit. You

should not be surprised at my saying, 'You must be born again.'
The wind blows wherever it pleases. You hear its sound, but you
cannot tell where it comes from or where it is going. So it is with
everyone born of the Spirit.]

Nicodemus is struggling with the "Nicodemus complex". Though Jesus is trying to plainly articulate to Nicodemus the Kingdom reality, he is snared by his cursed world mentality. He is trapped in the old or fallen paradigm of Adam so he is unable to grasp the Kingdom concept. He was still trying to 'physically' comprehend divine things and it only led to further frustration.

This happens when we try to fit Heavenly concepts into earthly concepts. Nothing in God's Word is written with logic or human reasoning in mind. Many of us have a "Nicodemus complex" about something God called us to do. Like Nicodemus we just don't see how we can fit into God's divine plan to prosper us beyond our imagination. Notice, Jesus tells Nicodemus that you can't even understand me because we don't come from the same place and we don't speak the same language (author paraphrase). Remember that language is one of the main cultural blocks of cultural influence.

So if Nicodemus is speaking a different language than Jesus, he is most certainly thinking with a different thought pattern than Jesus. That is the "fallen" paradigm of Adam. Many Christians struggle with this today, because the ceiling of the cursed world mentality hinders individuals from being able to "see" the Kingdom or awaken to the perception of its actual and authentic existence within them. Jesus knew this that is why He explained to Nicodemus that he needed to be "born again." However, born again here is the Greek word "ano then." It means that a person must start from the beginning point, which Jesus is proposing isn't our mother's womb; it's the Spirit of God. He is saying "you need a new paradigm." Therefore being born again is the actual point at which one exchanges a fallen paradigm with the Kingdom paradigm. When you are awakened to your "original starting point," you have awakened the sleeping giant within and greatness is about to be unleashed.

You see if you're going to break out of the fallen paradigm of Adam, you first need to realize where you began. Understand you began as a spirit; that you are a spirit, and a speaking spirit. Realize that God cut you out of the fabric of His eternal and unlimited being to establish you with that same unhindered reality. Don't allow a defeated and limited self-perception to hold your true God hunger hostage. You must realize this truth of God's unlimited nature in you and hunger after it with all you have.

Nicodemus' hunger wasn't after God's Kingdom; it was still being fed by worldly concepts and philosophies. When this happens, our approach to the Kingdom is off and we find ourselves much like Nicodemus talking to Jesus, feeling as though we are having two totally separate conversations with Him. Hunger for God's Word always leads to correct alignment with the path of truth. God promises that if we acknowledge Him first in our life, (seek after, search and hunger for) He'll make sure our paths are smooth, even the crooked ones we sometimes encounter (Proverbs 3:6).

This is His divine adjustment in our hearts, causing us to walk in alignment with His Kingdom. Like Nicodemus, all must be born again, and began to take off our old self, habits, and erroneous ways of seeing God. Many Christians are like Nicodemus, Sunday after Sunday they are looking directly at Jesus (the Kingdom) but don't know how to approach Him. Often times people begin to wonder if God even hears their prayers.

We must change our concept of life and develop a new hunger that craves the eternal truth of Christ's Kingdom. That type of hunger cries out to God, "Teach me your ways." This insatiable hunger releases unlimited access to the throne. Though it can be difficult to maintain a genuine God-hunger in a godless world that surrounds us, we have to use our faith to keep us on the path of seeking, searching, and knocking until we receive all that God has promised to release in our lives. Matthew 5:6 reminds that *"Blessed is he who hungers and thirsts after righteousness for he will be filled."* We see here it's not just hunger that releases and gives us access to the blessing; it's a hunger after God's "righteousness." Righteousness means alignment with law. We have to hunger after the King's laws, His way of doing things, because where His divine law lies is where His heart is also. A healthy spiritual hunger will always lead us directly to the birthing place of God's heart.

Some practical steps you can began to take to cultivate a healthy spiritual diet begins with examining your daily habits, conversations, and examining how they may or may not be influencing us in the direction of the kind of spiritual appetite we should have.

Take the time to really ruminate on your answers and begin to examine the impact that outer influences may be having on your overall hunger and pursuit of God's Kingdom.

What is your spiritual diet? Take a few moments to note some of the words and actions you feed on during your day.

Think about one conversation you had today. Summarize it.

_____
_____
_____
_____

What made you choose this conversation? Was it uplifting?

_____
_____
_____
_____

What are your can't miss television programs?

_____
_____
_____
_____

Watch those programs with a pen in your hand and note the many messages that they may be intentionally or unintentionally sending you. Why do you like this show? How does this show feed you?

_____
_____
_____
_____

What kind of music do you listen to? What is your favorite song?

_____
_____

Listen to your favorite songs and pick out a few verses. Why do you think you like this genre of music?

What do you like most about these songs? How do you feel about other people and yourself as you listen to them? (Ex: empowered, emotional, sexy, spiritually connected to the Lord)

How does your song choice reflect you as a person?

Remember this about training about your hunger. As you train your "hunger" towards the Lord you are actually guiding your steps and your movements. You are actually setting directions for yourself, for your life and other lives you may touch. You are actually mapping the course for your future.

So you want to train your hunger. You want to train it to seek Godly wisdom, to search for the keys that unlock heaven. You want to put away childish things and put on the full armor of Christ. You want to be nourished by the Word and the Spirit of His Kingdom.

Kingdom Keys:

1. When you hear gossip do not participate in the conversation. Refuse to participate in it. Walk away or calmly interject something positive into the conversation to steer it away from negativity.

2. Record a Sunday lecture or purchase one from your pastor or another minister. Listen to it in your car or while you are cleaning or whenever you would normally listen to music or watch television.

3. Find a gospel CD that reflects the musical style that interests you. You'd be surprised at how much good music there is out there that glorifies God.

4. Your thoughts and ideas:

_____
_____
_____
_____
_____
_____
_____

Our prayer: Lord, fill me up with that which you love to keep me from that which you do not love.

Our actions: Dedicate at least one hour a day to studying God's Word. Write down a verse from the Bible.

_____

_____

_____

_____

_____

_____

How can you bring this verse to life in your life?
Record your experience.

_____

_____

_____

_____

_____

_____

_____

_____

9

The Law of Expectation: The Framework of Excellence

"High achievement always takes place in the framework of high expectation."—Charles F. Kettering, American engineer, inventor of the electric starter

The Future's Framework

From the beginning God had an overwhelming expectation of you and me. He imagined what we would be like, how we'd look and the kind of life we would experience. His intentions flowed from His sovereign ability and grace to design after His own kind. His power to create and build were simply the platforms for His success. God had an extreme sense and power of expectation that would not allow Him to consider any limitations for our existence; the power that lies in Himself, the image of the Creator, which He sought to produce in us since the beginning. He continued to imagine and orchestrate every tiny detail of our future living condition. In this, God Himself became familiar with the idea of us and through His unlimited imagination and expectation for us.

His love, mercy and compassion sprang forth like springs of water. He never limited our abilities; instead He gave us all the creative and unique power He possessed by investing it into our divine nature and being. This creativity still lives in you and I today.

We can breathe with power into the future of our existence through words, power thinking and thoughts of life. Our lives are the result of what we truly expect daily. You can live in that expectation as it is genetically built into our spiritual DNA. That means the champion within you exists, never defeated, and carries that same mentality of the almighty Creator. You have the power to succeed by tapping into that inner champion!

The winner inside of you knows the power that lies beneath and is waiting to be unleashed through victorious thoughts, habits and beliefs. You cannot have a defeated mentality, the creative and winning power of the King exists inside of you. Breathe with expectation into your life and future. Design your life the way you imagine and see it. Develop your thoughts into power sources of expectation that you release through declarations, prayers of faith and healthy conversations. Your future is depending on your expectation. The theme of your life is created through the thoughts and ideas in which you become familiar. The more time you spend with these positive ideas of your life, just like God, the picture of your future becomes a clearer image. Soon, you'll be living in that picture because you will have framed your world through power of expectation.

Expectation Always Wins

Victorious living always begins with the way we choose to view ourselves in life. If we are going to break free from the normal limitations of our present realities, then who we truly see when we look in the mirror is going to have to change . . . fast! This is important because our self-image will always be the determinate of our future success. Expectation is the framework of that success.

As long as anyone goes through life with a defeated perspective of who they are, they'll always feel as though they are losing battles instead of winning them. This can be frustrating, to feel as though you *can't get a break* in life. You may be able to relate to this experience. For years growing up in church I was always taught that Christianity was the victorious life. I would always hear common phrases being shouted in songs such as, "The devil is under our feet!" or, "We've got the victory!" Yet, as I examined the lives of so many saints there were signs of defeat everywhere.

Many believers have this same experience today. When in the church house they seem bold, excited and vibrant about living; however, when they leave the church, it's a different story and the exuberance they had before tends to slip away. Soon, as the reality of their current situations set in, discouragement begins to show its face and the spirit of defeat and failure arise. Soon after, the same person who seemed to be excited and vibrant on Sunday morning quickly becomes defenseless and discouraged by Tuesday night.

Most Christians have been taught how to be victorious inside the church walls, but not how to succeed outside of them.

What happened? Well, for starters, most Christians have been taught how to be victorious inside the church walls, but not how to succeed outside of them.

Most Christians have been taught how to be victorious inside the church walls, but not how to succeed outside of them.

They have a defeated mentality of themselves. They haven't been trained to cultivate a winning mentality or a constant expectation for life. Neither have they been taught how to take the necessary action to produce the harvest they desire to possess. Most teaching in the church paints a distorted image of Christian living, as though what takes place one day a week in the church house is somehow enough to create the positive lasting change we need throughout the week.

This type of thinking only teaches people to believe that if they just "wait on the Lord" they will get the things they want in life.

I have found that we rarely get what we *want* out of life, rather we often get what we *expect*. We get what we are willing to put a demand on, take action on and pursue with all of our hearts. "Want" can create a burning desire on the inside while "expectation" will always inspire you to action. Therefore, wanting and expecting something are two totally different ideas.

For years I have witnessed many people who want to be healed, pray to be healed, but continue in the same attitudes, thought patterns and behaviors. As a result they see no changes in their bodies and many times their situation worsens. This is because often times individuals will ask for something but they don't have a real expectation of receiving it.

Faith is a choice and being healed, or overcoming any negative obstacle, is a product of the decision we first have to make in our hearts. We must decide that we've already overcome and that we are simply looking forward to the manifestation. Once we decide to overcome and receive by faith, expectation naturally emerges from the inside and we will begin to look forward to positive outcomes.

When our expectation is fully active it impacts the way we operate in circumstances. It influences the way we think, function, and determines the action we are willing to take to produce those positive outcomes. When used correctly, expectation can be one of the most powerful forces we experience in life.

Why is expectation so powerful? Expectation is powerful because it is more than a word or spiritual concept; it is a divine spiritual law in the Kingdom. Expectation trains the heart and mind of the believer to begin to "realize" that they've already overcome and obtained their promise by faith. It encourages an anticipative attitude toward succeeding and possessing whatever they've believed for. It is impossible to tap into real expectation and stand still waiting on a harvest. Expectation gradually pushes the heart of the believer into the direction of divine opportunity and favor because it is tuned by the Spirit of God's reality.

Remember, the harmonious agreement of faith and expectation work together to create and actualize what's really yours to secure that Blessing and promise. At times your faith may lead you down a road that your natural mind cannot comprehend. Expectation then flows from the endless supply of Heaven's resource and abundance, therefore testifying to your heart that what you have believed in actually exists!

In God's mind there is a solution for everything, even the worst situation you may find yourself in. You have to believe this in order for His principles and laws to work for you. Now, I want you to understand that from out of God's mind everything seen and unseen has been established. It is from the boundless circumference of God's eternal imagination and creativity that you were also formed. This simply means you were created out of the same infinite place from which God created His supernatural law: His mind.

Therefore, expectation emerges from the law of God's endless creativity and once activated in our heart it ministers from that endless place allowing our faith to break us out of the normal confines of this world's system and into the realm of limitless opportunity. Expectation, being one of God's creative sources, isn't aware of any limitations that exist. You need to understand that this is exactly how God sees you. That same expectation flows through us, by His Spirit, giving us validity and permission to believe the seemingly "unbelievable" and do the seemingly "impossible."

Hebrews 11:1-2:

> *[Now, faith is being sure of what is [hoped for] and certain of what we do not see.]*

The expression "hoped for" has been commonly viewed as an idea of desperation and pity. The westernized view of this word has taken the impact out of its true meaning. The word is "expect" in the Greek, and means to have an intense and eager anticipation; to confidently look for. So then faith is being sure with an intense expectation for something to (physically) happen. This expectation is not like expectation in the world, hoping for something that may or may not happen. That isn't an option with the law of expectation.

The believer's expectation emerges from a sure guarantee and promise in God's Word that He is faithful and His Word is already established, bringing to pass what we've set our hearts on. When you've tapped into true expectation you'll never accept "no" when it comes to any of God's promises. Why? Because you'll understand that God's Word is His unlimited promise to you waiting to bear fruit in the lives of faith-filled expecting believers. God designed it that way. He wants to express His limitless power through our lives so that people will know His Kingdom is a kingdom without ends. As a result of expectation operating in your life, you should always be getting increasingly better in your health, emotions, and finances. God wants every area of our lives to testify of His goodness and His spiritual reality, where no limitations exist.

You should keep this as a life motto and at the forefront of your heart: "no limitations exist for me in Heaven, therefore none exist for me in the earth." Meditate on it day and night and feed from this truth in every realm of your life. You are not limited. Your life is the result of Christ's finished work on the cross, in which He defied every human limitation possible. Stop allowing people to tell you what you can and cannot do. I am telling you that as a legal citizen of the Kingdom, you possess all rights and lawful authority to live outside of the earth's system and its boundaries. Take your eyes off what you see because common statistics don't apply to you.

Ascension Power

Though the flesh may have its limits, you must remember that you are not being called to live out of your mortal body. Remember, you are the "body of Christ." That means every obstacle, hindrance and limitation that Jesus overcame in this life, you've already overcame by faith in His death, resurrection and ascension. Revelation 12:11 reminds us: [*"They overcame him by the blood of the Lamb and by the word of their testimony."*]

You've already overcome in Christ. Think about that! That's your winning testimony; you are His body and by faith in Him, you have joined in His victory on the cross! Jesus broke the limitations for you. Your only responsibility is to not pick them back up.

Jesus broke the limitations for you. Your only responsibility is to not pick them back up.

The idea is commonly held that *"Christ in us"* is simply a metaphor or colorful phrase. It's

> **Jesus broke the limitations for you. Your only responsibility is to not pick them back up.**

not; it is conceptual and it is reality. It is a supreme truth that you are to live out of every day of your life. Every day I experience life above its normal boundaries. You know, I never take *no* for an answer, nor do I allow anyone to tell me what I can and cannot accomplish. In my mind I truly believe that I am a part of Christ's risen body, so if no limits exist for Him, then none exist for me either. I am always eager to see God bring His Word to pass.

Now, when I say *eager* I am not referring to being anxious or desperate. What I mean is I am so convinced that God cannot fail that I am always leaning over to see the manifestation of His promises. This is called living out of your "ascended place". When Jesus rose and ascended into Heaven He brought us, His body, with Him. When God placed all things under His feet, He placed them under our feet too. He recovered all that man lost through the fall of Adam, giving us permission to once again operate out of our unlimited God-nature within. Through His Kingdom, God is gradually restoring us back to that place. We have to focus on being His body in the earth and not our own.

Ideas like this are called *"kingdom concepts"* given to us by God to help us grasp the reality and enhance our awareness of His Kingdom in us and increase our expectation to manifest it. It is only through these Kingdom concepts and ideas that we are able to clearly see the picture of God's power within us and that the limits of this flesh are weakened, losing its power and control over our lives. The Word teaches us that we have been *"raised and seated with Christ in Heavenly realms"* (Ephesians 2:6). It is from this exalted place Paul that encourages also us to adjust our thoughts, wills and actions in Colossians 3:1-2:

> *[Since then you have been seated with Christ, set your hearts on things above, where Christ is seated at the right hand of God. Set your mind on things above, not on earthly things. For you died and your life is now hidden in Christ. When Christ who is your life appears, then you also will appear with him in glory.]*

This literally means the majority of our day should be spent thinking about Heavenly things, God's promises, and His abundant blessings. *"Your life,"* meaning the normal and average life you experienced before Christ, is long gone. You have His life to live out of now. I know this can be hard to picture but this is where your expectation of power and abundance flow.

Setting your desires and thoughts on this truth allows you to escape the doubt, fear and the hindrances of your present reality. We can live out of a higher reality, never again moved or swayed by the operations of this world. The power of the law of expectation rests in the sure reality of Heaven's power and its unlimited promises given to you through faith in Christ.

Take into account this example: A pilot spends most of his time in the sky defying the laws of gravity. So then naturally his attention is focused more on elements above the earth, rather than below it. If a pilot is going to succeed at what he does, he can't spend his time thinking about what is happening on the ground or beneath him. His concentration must be geared toward the laws of aviation, weather conditions, wind turbulences, and other functions that take place above the clouds. It is no different for believers. As we are the body of an ascended Savior, we have to adjust our thoughts and philosophies to ideas and concepts that supersede the basic thought patterns of this world.

We have to learn to think and live from our seated place on the throne in Heaven, which begins with focusing and concentrating our thoughts on the limitless promises of God. Otherwise we are limiting God's ability to influence our lives because we haven't agreed with and actualized His spiritual laws. It doesn't matter how ridiculous some of God's promises may sound. They are supposed to sound that way; they are concepts above the world. As I mentioned before, God has called us to spiritual aviation.

Think about this: when you look at a building from the ground up, it seems huge and extremely high. However, if you take the elevator to the roof, walk to the edge of it and look down, your perspective will have changed. Things seem a lot smaller than they did when you were at the bottom. That is what happens when we yield our daily thoughts to the limitless imaginations of God's Word. As we concentrate and focus on Christ's ascended reality, we realize all the more that we are seated above, in Heavenly places. By taking on Heavenly concepts we can began to view circumstances in our life from the top down instead of from the bottom up. Once you grasp this concept, you realize that things are not as big or as bad as they once seemed, and that you have already risen to the top!

By learning to develop your "ascended mindset" you are escaping the limitations of this world. Through the force of expectation, you are now consciously tapping into one of God's most powerful laws. Fear loses its deadly grip where expectation is presently active. Doubt cannot dwell in the presence of such superior law. Both must die or become inactive, in the presence of such greater truth.

Guarding your Expectation

As previously mentioned, the same way gravity must yield to the law of lift, the laws of this cursed world system must yield to the laws of God's Kingdom. Through this "new mindset" God wants to change your attitude about yourself and life. His expectation will produce a confidence of manifestation and stubbornness not to accept anything less than what God says about your situation. When this kind of expectation is present, faith becomes full-blown and miracles are sure to happen. Only when we allow the physicality of our present condition to influence our belief systems do we lose that expectation.

When unbelief is entertained, slowly but surely our confidence in what God has said begins to slip away. That is why it is so important for us to be watchful of who we share our dreams with, who we listen to, and who we allow to speak into our lives. Especially during difficult times, we need to be mindful of what comes into our ear and eye gates. Conversely, we need to be protective of what expectations we have. When the voices that we listen to do not line up with what we know God has spoken to us, we must totally cut them off from our lives. It is so important that we grasp this principle.

> When unbelief is entertained, slowly but surely our confidence in what God has said begins to slip away. That is why it is so important for us to be watchful of who we share our dreams with, who we listen to, and who we allow to speak into our lives.

When unbelief is entertained, slowly but surely our confidence in what God has said begins to slip away.

That is why it is so important for us to be watchful of who we share our dreams with, who we listen to, and who we allow to speak into our lives.

Holding on to your own expectation can be a battle. Even in expectant times, understand that negative forces will continue to attack your mindset in order to steal Godly ideas and concepts. You may feel like you believe God for something, but as time passes and situations arise, you are finding it more and more difficult to hang on to your expectation. It is our responsibility as citizens of the Kingdom to activate the law of expectation, become totally dependent on what the King has promised us, and then hold on to it.

How do we activate and walk in our expectation? How do we maintain it once we have accessed it? Here are 5 keys to help you activate and remain confident in what God has promised you:

1. Repetition in the Word—The Word of God is actually the King's law spoken and given to us to learn, meditate on, and put into active perpetuation in our lives. Since God is the supreme and sovereign ranking King in the universe, no law supersedes His Word. If we can learn to become consistent in meditating on it and applying it, its divine pattern will become alive to us, and by living out its truths we can continually defy the limitations of this world. The Greek word for faith is "pistis," which means persuasion. One of the ways we create this persuasion is by rehearsing the promises of God in regards to our circumstance. Remind yourself every day and night what you are entitled to according to the King's law. Now, you have to actually commit to doing this every day and night. Joshua 1:8 clearly reiterates the truth that God's promises must be meditated on and confessed night and day. For only then will we become successful and prosperous in God's Kingdom. As royal citizens of Heaven, we are not just promised the things in God's Word. Within God's Word we have inherited entitlements and benefits guaranteed to

us, if we are willing to apply faith to them. When you do this you are training your spirit only to expect what is written in God's law and nothing else.

2. Get a greater understanding of God's word — The main purpose for understanding is to increase your perceived value of the Word. You will not be repetitive about something you don't see the value in, so it is important that as you rehearse the Word, you ask the Holy Spirit to give revelation of His law so that the reality of its value and possible impact in your life is revealed to you.

3. Say what you expect out loud — As humans we have an inner ear and an outer ear. Both work together to transmit information to our central nervous system. Confessing the Word out loud reinforces its reality. Job 22:28 reminds us of our ability inherited through Jesus' blood to actually decree what we want to see in our lives based on the Word. This is intended to train our minds to expect exactly what is said.

4. Find testimonies and stories of real people who have overcome or accomplished what you are trying to do — Real life experiences are one of the best convincers to us that if someone else can do it, we can. Use the Internet to search for people of great accomplishment, particularly in the area you are trying to achieve. Finding individuals in the Bible who relate to the area of faith in which you are being challenged is also a great way to tap into a greater level of expectation. God's laws will work for you just as they did for them.

5. Cut off negative people — Make the decision to eradicate negative, doubtful, and unsupportive people from your life. These people are only weighing you down and poisoning your faith with unbelief. Don't allow people to speak against the Word in your heart. Build your relationships around people who support you, believe in you, and will stand and expect with you no matter what it is! This also means basing your relationships around faith-filled, faith-talking and faith-walking people. Two cannot walk together

unless they agree and you cannot rise above your relationships. You are what you hand around. Do not be unequally yoked believer with non-believers. Look at it this way: not choosing to build relationships with those who expect the same things out of the Kingdom as you do is spiritual suicide.

God's expectation of our victory is a reflection of His ability and power that He has invested into us through His internal government. Just because things around us do not agree right away with what we say or believe doesn't mean that we accept those circumstances. Regardless of what this dark and negative world has tried to reinforce to you, you can live in its system and not be subject to it. The Kingdom of Heaven is a higher reality and the kingdom of this world is an inferior one. Essentially the results you get will be dependent upon which reality that you choose to subject yourself to.

The truth is in God's eyes. It's not over until you lay hold of what you have been expecting. This kind of faith and expectation never goes unnoticed, because nothing you do ever do in faith will ever go unrewarded by God. Life in this fallen world demands that we be stubborn about our divine promises and inheritance. We must hold on to them with all courage and diligence. It takes courage to remain positive and steadfast in God's Word when things around you are falling apart. Your problems often times in life are resilient so you have to be as well.

Our expectation is a combination of all these things that drives us to continue taking great leaps of faith that go beyond our own ability with the expectation that God will soon cut Himself in and cause our reality to shift! This is living victoriously. Not allowing your circumstances to dictate the end to you is the difference between being the victim and the victor. Remember that God's expectation of your success is not based on your ability but rather His own strength and power that He has placed inside of you through His unlimited Kingdom.

10

Unleashing God's Favor: Keys to Increased Living

"I will look on you with favor and make you fruitful and increase your numbers, and I will keep my covenant with you."
(Leviticus 26:9)

Winning Favor

The life you deserve lies in the freedom of God's abundant grace and His unmerited favor. Freedom begins within your heart and also the mentality that you can create change no matter your circumstances. You must recognize that regardless of the time and season you're always positioned for a turnaround and your power position in Christ's Kingdom makes any turnaround possible.

You cannot live the new life God has predestined for you still listening to the negative voices that echo from of your past or while remaining subject to a negative image you have of yourself. Your attitude must be continually and completely centered on the concept and reality of having a breakthrough mentality, which is the mindset that overcoming is simply a matter of tapping into your pre-designed pattern to succeed. You have to condition your thought life based on the core principle that the pattern to succeed is a blueprint built into your creation, and as you actualize its existence in you, you'll draw more and more from its unlimited substance.

There is a plan to win for each and every one of us, as mentioned in chapter one. We just need to learn how to tap into it. Once you've discovered this Kingdom truth and committed to it, you'll always be aware of the inner strength you possess to break out of every negative and reoccurring cycle in your life.

You have the unlimited power and favor of God resting upon you. You may or may not realize it, but His unlimited favor and grace are safely transitioning you through every season you experience. No matter the situation, you can expect favor. When you plan for favor you plan to win. You're planning for God to lift you above every law of limitation and gravitational pull of this cursed world reality. Expect that favorable lift to gradually open doors for you that you previously couldn't see.

Expecting God's favor places your feet on the path of acceleration, giving you an advantage over all of your competition. With this winning favor you can expect the unexpected, believe the unbelievable and do the impossible. It's not your ability; it's God's amazing grace abounding in every area to propel you to destiny. You can win by tapping into favor and using God's supernatural ability to supersede any circumstance. Life's limitations are no match for a God-endorsed life.

When you have God speaking favorably about you, over you, and for you, men will turn their hearts to you and doors will open.

> **When you have God speaking favorably about you, over you, and for you, men will turn their hearts to you and doors will open.**

When you have God speaking favorably about you, over you, and for you, men will turn their hearts to you and doors will open. Even if they don't open immediately just keep declaring, "I have the favor of God in me and it's opening every avenue to me." Don't limit your expectation of what God's favor can do for you. Believe that you will prosper. Demand it and prepare to advance as supernatural favor continues to bring supernatural growth.

The power to break through lies in your ability to tap into the favor and plan God has divinely invested into you through His Word.

You've Been Approved

God's favor on you is His sign of approval. Sometimes as God's children we wonder if God is actually pleased with us, or if He really approves of our lives. The answer is yes, He really is. God is pleased with you, regardless of how you may feel or the things you may have done. To show you how much He approves of you He sealed you with the sign of His favor and Spirit. That's why it says in Ephesians 1:13: *[When you believed, you were marked in him with a seal (of approval), the promised Holy Spirit].*

A [government] seal is a stamp engraved with a signature or emblem representing that government. Seals were originally used in ancient kingdoms to gather both sides of a government document with a seal-like clasp engraved with a government symbol. Entry into the scroll was impossible without breaking the seal. It was an embossment designed to represent that kingdom. It means official, authentic and signed with the king's approval. That seal is the key to receiving whatever the king has placed in that document.

In Exodus 28:6-14, you will find that on the garment of the high priest there were two royal seals on the shoulders of his garment. That royal seal was an embossment engraved with names of the sons of Israel. In this sense, Isaiah was correct when he said, "the government will be on *his* shoulders." (Isaiah 9:6) As Christ is the *Head*, and we are His *body*. We are then His shoulders and therefore the government is upon us. This is an expression used to communicate the extension of His sovereign ruling power extended to us in the earth. So you see, in the same way we have been impressed, or sealed, with the sign of the Holy Spirit giving us access to the inheritance of Jesus' throne.

I want to make it clear that whenever a king puts his royal stamp on anything, he is establishing it as official property of his kingdom. By his seal of approval he is saying, *"I am endorsing this with my name."* That government seal was sometimes engraved on a signet ring, worn by the king or his royal officials. The ring was then impressed into official documents in order to authenticate them.

The seal-making process involved heavy labor, molding the impression of the government symbol in a circular or round piece of metal. You are impressed with that seal. Through His son's Spirit, God's impression is in your heart. And His favor and approval are all the power you need to advance with excellence and achievement.

There is something interesting that takes place in John 3:16-17. Christ was sealed with God's approval when He was baptized in water by John. John was afraid to baptize Jesus as he felt lower than Him. However Jesus' response was incredible, and should serve as a sign to every Christian the authentic power He has given us through His favor.

> *[Jesus was baptized too. And as he was praying, heaven was opened and the Holy Spirit descended on him in bodily form like a dove. And a voice came from heaven: "You are my Son, whom I love; with you I am well pleased."]* (Luke 3:22)

Now, carefully observe that it says after Jesus came out of the water the Holy Spirit descended upon Him like a dove in "bodily form." Meaning what they saw was another person in human-like form stepping into Jesus. Soon after, the voice of the Lord spoke and He said, *"This is my son, in whom I am well pleased."*

The word *pleased* also means *"one's approval."* When God says *"in whom I love"* that phrase can literally be translated *"favor."* This means Jesus was stamped with the royal seal of favor and approved by the Holy Governor (Spirit) who claims us as children of the inheritance. This is why Jesus told John that in order for *"all righteousness"* to be fulfilled, he had to baptize Him. *Righteousness* is total alignment with God's perfect law; meaning there existed a righteousness John was not aware of, and Jesus was about to fulfill it in that moment. That righteousness was the law of sonship that can only be achieved through the Blessing of God's Spirit. (Although Jesus was one with the Spirit, He had to show us the grace of sonship.)

God's Spirit of love and favor are His seal of approval and advancement. God isn't denying you; He is claiming you before all of Heaven and earth. What God is saying about you is that His name is on you and He has endorsed you. When He placed His seal upon you, there was a voice that went out from the Heaven saying, *"You are my son, whom I favor and I approve of you."*

God has endorsed your life, and by placing a conscious demand on His favor, you are moving into the divine opportunity He has prepared for you. You are approved!

Don't let anyone discourage you from relying on and believing in the abundance of God's favor He has sealed you with in your heart. You, like Jesus, have been impressed with the person of the Holy Spirit. He is our signed and sealed government proof that we are truly official sons of the King. This makes us royalty and gives us full governing power in our Father's Kingdom to exercise in the earth. Look at Romans 14:16:

> *[For you did not receive a spirit that makes you a slave again to fear, but you received the Spirit of sonship. And by him we cry, "Abba, Father." The Spirit himself testifies with our spirit that we are God's children. Now if we are children, then we are heirs — heirs*

of God and co-heirs with Christ, if indeed we share in his sufferings in order that we may also share in his glory.]

Our inheritance includes the full benefits of God's Heavenly government. Again, we see here that the Holy Spirit is testifying on our behalf that we are truly sons of God. He's saying to us, *"You are legitimate sons of the Kingdom."* It's our job to believe and mediate on this truth day and night. Fear is not something what we received from God. We did not receive an insecure, abandoned and fatherless spirit; we received full power of Heaven's throne. Our identities are wrapped up in the increase of favor God has lavished upon us through His throne. That's why we have to become "Throne Thinkers." A Throne Thinker has actualized his favor with the King as son and royal servant of His government.

So, what does having the royal authority in Heaven to rule with look like in our personal and everyday lives? Well, first, we have to walk in the mentality of Christ's internal Kingship; otherwise no one else is going to recognize our grace. It starts with you, your mind and subduing it to this thought and idea: "I am a royal son, sealed and approved by my Father the King." Start saying this to yourself daily until a clear image of who you are as a son of Heaven becomes the inner picture you have of yourself.

Your inheritance depends on your ability to become one with this truth. This is where your identity lies, in the truth that Christ, ruler of all creation, has endowed you with the same splendor to share in His abundant Kingship. That's the power of living a God-endorsed life. God's favor is on you throughout every season, testifying to this same truth.

Even when you feel limited or begin doubting yourself, don't entertain it. God is still saying, "I have endorsed you with my favor to succeed." Any thought that doesn't line up with that truth didn't come from God. You have the power to break through; every limitation must yield to the presence of God's intrinsic favor.

Every person you meet and every connection you make will be empowered with the energy of God's favor resting upon you. They won't be able to describe or articulate it. All they'll know is that there is something really special about you and they'll be drawn to that flow of positive energy. The favor of God is like a scent, or an aroma you give off gently whispering to those you meet, "He is a son of God." With this God-endorsed favor you can expect the Blessing, open doors, and future success.

Expect people to begin to align with you from different places, even the ones that didn't want to agree with you before. As you begin to apply force to this supernatural grace, you will see people will began to respond to you differently because you will have responded to yourself in a whole new way. Favor, grace and increase are all yours through the seal of approval of God's claim on your life.

The Science of Breakthrough

As mentioned earlier in chapter five, grace is also the extension of God's favor dwelling in you. Grace exists to release the authentic and tangible energy of God's unlimited potential. That favor is succeeding without sweat. When favor invades your life it allows you to break into the dormant potential of the Creator that's resting inside of you. You can rely on His power and ability to reshape your life. The power to live, create, and function in a realm that exists high above life's limitations is from the unmerited favor of God lifting you above every circumstance in life. Grace unlocks that power, enabling the potential within in you to succeed with ease. Favor is that winning potential.

Often times you're one person away from walking into your destiny or obtaining that promise you've been waiting on. Favor is like an energy source that can connect you to the right people in the right places at the right time. Releasing God's favor is the way to ensure victory over every problem, obstacle and circumstance. Using God's favor to turn your life around begins with a mentality that you were born to succeed and not lose. What I mean is, deprogramming bad thoughts and ideas that nothing good ever seems to happen for you or that you just can't get a break. When the Blessing is on you it reminds you that you're favored by God and strapped with supernatural power to increase in whatever you put your hand to.

The secret to releasing this favor lies in this truth, just like any supernatural law: it is untapped potential waiting in the basement of our souls to be ignited, harnessed, and released through applying faith daily. Sometimes what you're waiting for is right underneath you, waiting for you to claim possession of it.

The Word of God is your title deed guaranteeing your inheritance of God's Blessing. This means in order to use grace to create the turnaround you desire to see, you must always position and posture yourself with an expectation for breakthrough. Often times, individuals can become so tied up with the winds of life's storms that they begin to focus more on coming out rather than preparing to come out. If we want the victory Christ has pre-designed for us, then a mentality of preparation is imperative. You will only be able to benefit from what you've prepared for. See, when you have advantageous favor working for you, you should always be conscious of the fact that some form of breakthrough is always available in every season. Your time to overcome has been here since Jesus died on that cross over 2,000 years ago. If you never expect it, then you'll never prepare to see God's plan manifest in your life.

Often times, individuals can become so tied up with the winds of life's storms that they begin to focus more on coming out rather than preparing to come out.

You see, God's plan is still the same. His plan is to heal you and heal the land. Your brokenness doesn't make you ineligible for the Blessing, it makes you a perfect candidate for breakthrough. You have to understand that God's idea of healing is full restoration; putting everything back the way it was. That's what the Blessing does; it automatically puts things back in their original place.

That's what turnaround really is: tapping into God's original plan for every season of your life. You have favor for breakthrough and the creative power of God inside of you. Tap into it! This means that you have the ability to create new seasons with new words. That's the power of God's creativity within you.

His favor will go forth with your words to create new opportunities and open up doors in new places. The Spirit of recovery was invested into you with Christ's Spirit. This should be your demeanor; that you're always one step away from victory. Please, understand that you're never so deep in a spiritual pit that you don't have the divine power to break yourself out. The Blessing is your total recovery package, along with your promise of newness, healing and turnaround.

God's supernatural strength within is flowing with abundance waiting to create shift in any area you desire to see it. Remember, as long as you have favor, breakthrough is always right around the corner and new beginnings are just a few words away. Begin to say that to yourself: *"My new beginnings are just around the corner."*

A Double Portion of Favor

There are two types of favor: favor with God (spiritual blessing) and favor with man (earthly blessing). You can use them both to influence with the Kingdom of God. Grace always positions you to do what others say you can't. That's because you have both sides of God's unlimited plan working for you. On one side, the spiritual side, you have all of God's tangible energy flowing within you. You can tap into it at any time, giving you the authority to speak into the unseen to produce a harvest in the natural.

Our breakthrough power is unlimited when you realize that all spiritual blessings in Christ have been given to us. (Ephesians 1:3). We are crowned with that spiritual favor. We can change things with powerful prayer, positive words, and the supernatural wisdom of God. If we don't learn to value this double portion of favor on us, we'll lose the value and impact of having it in our lives.

On the other side of grace, you have favor with man. This kind of favor will cause you to make the right connections. Though people may not say it, they will be thinking *"What is it about this person?"* That's the supernatural influence of God's favor witnessing to the conscience of man that you are someone worthy of honor. Favor will cause man to honor you because God has honor.

I remember my first year in the sales industry. I was told not to expect to earn more than $28,000 my first year because of my inexperience. I was also told that it would be impossible to earn in the $60,000-80,000 income bracket since I didn't have the enough clientele to create what's called "repeat and referral" business (the ability to gain clientele from existing clients.) The favor in me wouldn't let me accept that. I knew I was not bound to that limitation because I had favor with the King of the universe, and He knows everybody. And because I had favor with God, I naturally found favor with man.

I began to call in clientele and repeat and referral business by declaring it out loud. My first month I didn't sell anything, the next month I made 3 sells, and then the next month only 9 sales. After that I began to wonder if I was in the right business, but the Spirit of favor reminded me I had been endorsed by God and not to give in or put down my faith. The next month I had the most sales in the company and made over $8,000. The rest from there was a snowball effect as I continued to increase in clientele. I ended up making over $75,000 my first year. What happened? I realized who I was in God and actualized the King's favor that was on my life. It helped me to increase my self-value, honor who I was, and put a demand on the divine ability within me. That divine favor naturally lifted me above the gravity of the limits that had been previously spoken to me.

I was able to supernaturally create a sustainable repeat and referral client base in the first year. God even allowed me to find favor with an entire family that referred almost 2-3 family members or friends to me each month! Not only that, I became good friends with a client of mine who happened to be a multi-millionaire from Alaska, and he was also responsible for helping me expand my business. You see, favor will take the frustration out of living and cause you to realize it's not you on your own, but the God-nature within pouring into every area of your life. You can escape the gravitational pull of negative words spoken about you by remaining focused on the supernatural grace that can overcome any odds, both spiritually and materially.

Overcoming Fear with Favor

Tapping into God's favor should release a constant reminder that it isn't just you journeying the path of life. God is with you every step of the way. The Spirit of favor knows and constantly acknowledges the presence of the King, and that He is constantly smiling upon you through every phase of life. That's why you can hold on to God's promises, securely and with a healthy perspective of how you see yourself. You can have surety of the incredible work God wants to accomplish through your life.

Faith works through favor, drawing from the grace of God's promises to encourage victory and overcoming power in your heart. Fear wants to stop that victory. Fear wants you to believe that God isn't going to do just what He has said. Fear wants you afraid that if you actually step out on faith and trust God's Word He somehow isn't going to come through for you and you'll be left looking like a fool. Don't let fear paralyze you. Take a stand!

When fear tries to creep in, your response has to be *"No, God favors me too much not bring His Word to pass!"* Defeat is not an option. Don't be timid and make the decision to settle or take whatever's thrown at you. Be firm in favor and speak favorably over every situation.

Be firm in favor and speak favorably over every situation.

> **Be firm in favor and speak favorably over every situation.**

The Time of God's Favor:

Luke 4:18-29

> *["The Spirit of the Lord is on me, because he has anointed me to proclaim good news to the poor. He has sent me to proclaim freedom for the prisoners and recovery of sight for the blind, to set the oppressed free, to proclaim the year of the Lord's favor." Then he rolled up the scroll, gave it back to the attendant and sat down. The eyes of everyone in the synagogue were fastened on him. He began by saying to them, "Today this scripture is fulfilled in your hearing."]*

The scripture above refers to a time during Jesus' ministry when He returned to Nazareth, the place of His birth. He was trying to help His people understand that the day they had been waiting for had finally come. In fact His exact words were, *"This scripture is fulfilled in your hearing today!"* When is the time of favor? The time of favor is here and it's now. This is God's awesome plan for you, that you be empowered with victory wherever you go at all times. The time for harvest is now. The sooner you realize it the closer you'll be to changing your outcomes. Your time of harvest is now! This is what Jesus wants you to understand.

Now is the time (or the season) of the Lord's favor. Everything in the Kingdom functions and operates in the now. You have the power of favor and increase today. You don't have to wait around hoping that God will bless you or that He will open doors for you. He's already given you all things. His supernatural favor is tuned by His will, and it's going to point you in the direction of divine opportunity. You won't stand in front of closed doors anymore. It's your time for favor, and God has already approved it! Break free from only thinking about what God will do in the future; release your faith and let Heaven impact your life now.

Ask yourself this question: "What will I do differently today than I did yesterday to produce different results in my life?" You can begin by filling your thoughts with the gift of God's present favor, and adjusting your words to what His promise says about you. You can begin expecting God to pay some bills off now. Expect Him to heal some hurts now. The foundation of the Kingdom is built on who God is and what He has already done. The Kingdom is not based on what or who He'll be. God is the great "I Am." God is His perfect law and the same perfect law produces the force of faith, which "is" the substance of what's hoped for. Everything in the Kingdom has now attached to it. Find out what yours is, and began to pursue the now reality that favor has unleashed over you.

The Law of Abundant Supply

Living a life without limits means that you understand how God desires to bless you with more than enough. The word "need" isn't in God's vocabulary, and is hardly His measuring stick for giving you anything. Need has nothing to do with it. God, in His nature, doesn't have the ability to supply only *enough*. When "just enough" keeps showing up in people's lives, there's still lack and those are traces of the cursed world system. Most times this occurs because they have placed limitations concerning God's ability to bless them. I often hear believers pray for what they need, not realizing they aren't speaking God's language. Consequently they become limited to their words and continue to survive instead of thrive.

If we are going to live in God's Kingdom and experience His elevated lifestyle we need to be clear on this one thing: *it is more than enough*. That is right, the lifestyle that the sovereign Kingdom of God produces is intended to produce more than enough in every sphere of your life, as God has already supplied our needs according to His riches.

Why then should we even talk to Him about need? As royalty in God's family our attitude needs to change from a begging mentality to an "I deserve" mentality. Our prayer life should be centered on God's thoughts, His limitless imagination and the inheritance of His Kingdom He has given us as His sons. Once we tap into His thoughts, the source of life, we can declare out of that secret place into every area of our life. When we tap into His concept of speaking and praying out of the realized unlimited and abundant place of Christ, the possibilities are endless to what we'll see manifest.

This is called "living out of the overflow." God's heart is the place of abundance and it is filled with a burning desire to increase you with no ends. This means by seeking God's heart you are naturally releasing overflow into your life. So no matter what, as God's royal family, birthed out of the secret place of His thoughts, there is a contract that exists to overflow your life with Heaven's riches and it's time to start expecting the reality of abundance everyday. He wants our cups to run over, so that people know how good He treats His family.

Recently after one my Kingdom Enrichment Seminars, I was approached by a lady who told me, "You know, as long as God gives me enough, I'll be fine with that." My first question was, "When you pay for something to eat, do you like it when the restaurant gives you just enough?" She responded, "No." My second question was, "When you pay for a hotel room are you pleased when there are just enough towels or necessities to accommodate you?" Again she said, "No." So I looked at her and asked, "Is there more you desire in your life?" Her answer was, "Yes."

In less than 2 minutes she contradicted everything she had just told me. Why? It was because she didn't really believe any of it. She was simply being bound to a limited mindset and way of thinking she had known her whole life.

Most people aren't trained to expect God's increase of abundance, as was the case with that particular lady. People who pretend they don't want abundance aren't being honest with themselves. The reason this woman, along with the rest of us, isn't pleased with just enough, is because God never designed us to live that way.

When the Kingdom occupies within us through the force of the Spirit, the complete image and characteristics of God are reactivated in us. This includes God's innate quality of overflow. Nothing in us ever says "just enough" once we come into Kingdom living. Once we accomplish one thing, the Holy Spirit has already given us another vision for next year, and then the next 10 years after that. Why? It is because God is the God of abundance. He doesn't know what enough is. His expectation for our lives is that we produce after His likeness, overflowing with increase until it pours out and impacts someone else's life.

The thought life of God consists of measureless quality, and He desires that same type of mindset for His children. Scripture after scripture reminds us of God's inability to produce just enough. The Bible never refers to God as "just enough."

Look at some of these verses concerning the laws of increase and abundance:

> Genesis 1:28: *[God blessed them and said to them, "Be fruitful and increase in number; fill the earth and subdue it.]*

> Deuteronomy 1:11: *[May the LORD, the God of your fathers, increase you a thousand times and bless you as he has promised!]*

> 2 Corinthians 9:10: *[Now he who supplies seed to the sower and bread for food will also supply and increase your store of seed and will enlarge the harvest of your righteousness.]*

> Isaiah 66:11: *[For you will nurse and be satisfied at her comforting breasts; you will drink deeply and delight in her overflowing abundance.]*

> Jeremiah 31:14: *[I will satisfy the priests with abundance, and my people will be filled with my bounty," declares the LORD.]*

> Psalm 66:12: *[You let men ride over our heads; we went through fire and water, but you brought us to a place of abundance.]*

(Note: These scriptures are great for powerful daily confessions.)

We can clearly see that God's plan is to produce nonstop abundance in whatever you put your hands to. This is the power of the Blessing; it makes rich and adds no sorrow with it. It only knows how to *add* things to your life. That Blessing is on you through Jesus Christ, and since you are His body, you are connected to an endless and supernatural supply.

Once God blesses you He doesn't have any intentions on stopping there. Sometimes individuals can be so enamored with what God has done for them that they place limitations on what He wants to do next. God's plan of increase doesn't only lie in how much He wants to give you. Increase also determines how fast something comes.

My father was raised on a farm in Holly Springs, Mississippi with 15 children. His life revolved around keeping watch over the animals and taking care of his father's crops. I once asked my grandmother why she had so many kids, and I asked if it was so that they could take care of the farm. Her reply was, "No." She said she was simply fertile and couldn't keep from having those kids. It was her fertility that caused the increase and continuous growth of her family.

This is how it is when favor is on us. We become fertile to receive and continually produce a harvest of abundance. That's the power of increase and it's been lavished on you in generous amounts. God is always looking to bring more to you and do more in your life, finances and family. You have to be sure that you don't limit Him to what He did the last time. If you have been doing this, begin dismantling that paradigm and cultivating a new mindset that "more" is okay with God. It is Kingdom and it is your destiny.

Speak favor and increase when you get up in the morning. Make the time to find scriptures that support God's promise of favor and begin applying them through positive confession over your health, family and finances. Begin saying, *"God, I put a lawful demand on favor and increase."* You should expect God to accelerate you beyond the normal confines of life. When you speak something you're going to begin to see it happen faster than what you expected. Increase goes beyond what you expect into the realm of God's unlimited resource which is His power to do exceedingly and abundantly above all you can ask or think (Ephesians 3:20). That's increase working through favor, because you are continually fertile with God's truth in every season to readily receive God's unlimited promises. Keep this at the front of your mind: *"I am increase, I am favor, I always increase and I always excel."*

Having favor doesn't always mean we tap into its abundance immediately. We have to learn that it's there and how to grow in it. Luke 2:52, says even Jesus "grew" in favor with God.

Here are 9 keys to growing in increase and favor abundance so that you can release the unlimited potential of Heaven's abundance:

1. Be prepared. God's favor can break you out of any season of adversity. You have to realize it first but also begin imagining yourself the way God sees you, as a king covered with the abundance of His grace. This is preparing your heart for turnaround. If you're conscious of this grace you'll know breakthrough is never far away. Prepare for increase, because what you prepare for is what you will get.

2. Stop watching other people. If you invest your time into comparing yourself to others you'll never see the value in what God has done in your life. This is truly a bad investment of your time that will only yield discouragement, envy and frustration. Watch God and His promise to put you on the path of victory. This will cause grace to explode as you realize you have the same ability as anyone to succeed at what you have geared you heart to.

3. Listen for God's voice. As you put a demand on divine favor, supernatural doors will immediately begin to open. You must have "eyes" to realize them or you will miss your divine opportunity. God will use His Spirit and voice of wisdom to guide you into the direction of favor He placed your blessing in.

4. Watch carefully, the plan will reveal itself. In God's blueprint is a plan to succeed. This plan often involves people and connections

God wants to make for you. You have to be attentive to where God wants you to go and who He wants you share your ideas with. You will soon see that regardless of what it is that you want to accomplish, God has already orchestrated a path for you to walk on that will lead you straight to your destiny. Favor is that plan and will give you the spiritual and mental edge you need to stay in alignment with Him. Gradually as you seek God for His strategy, the plan will make itself clear and you'll be walking in divine alignment to possess your inheritance of overflow.

5. Live the life you deserve in the promise of the Spirit. If God promised it to you, then it's yours no matter what. That promise is why you deserve favor, increase and Blessing. God, out of His own sovereignty and cognizance, made a promise to give you His Kingdom and a life of success. You have to realize it's yours by right, or you'll never feel you're good enough to receive His promises for your life. You deserve it. Always remember that.

6. Lift your standard. Change what you allow in your life. You have the power and authority to do so. Stop accepting, "No." Don't let people talk down to you. If someone doesn't honor your value, separate from them.

7. Expect beyond common standard. Your life wasn't meant to be normal or average. It was meant for more than common meaning. Remember that when you pray, make confessions and write out your dreams. Is your dream so big people have a hard time getting on board? If not, change it. Ask God to increase you and enlarge your vision.

8. Remember the time is perfect. Now is the time for favor. Put a relentless demand on it now and then measure the results.

9. Never stop expecting more. God can do more. He is not limited to what He did the last time. Always expect more than what you ask, because that's another plan of favor to always give you more than what you need.

This season is yours. Possess it. Your time is too valuable and precious to waste it doubting and entertaining limited ideas of the good that God wants to do in your life. There is no time to "wait around" hoping for a "turnaround." You have the power and favor within you to create your breakthrough. The King of kings has endorsed your life and you belong to His royal family. You are God-endorsed and God-approved! You are sealed with greatness, standing in the appointed time of favor and increase.

11

Heaven's Open Door Policy

*"Your gates shall remain open day and night so that men will bring you the wealth of the nations." —*Isaiah 60:11

Heavenly Transactions

One of the most important things for believers to understand about having the Kingdom of God within them is that God has given you His Kingdom so that you can live in an open Heaven. Isaiah puts it this way:

> *["Your gates shall remain open day and night so that men will bring you the wealth of the nations."]*

In Hebrew culture the gates represented a place of business or an area of commerce. At the gates were traveling business merchants bargaining and selling goods along with other marketplace activity. As long as the gates were open, the city was open for business. Gates are frequently used and referred to in the Bible. They have a significant meaning though. Beyond just being a place of business they represent a place of "transaction." In a Kingdom sense, this would mean "government transactions of Heaven."

You see, the Kingdom is a place of governing transactions. All the time and continuously around the clock, Heaven is moving and God is waiting to influence something in your life. In her book *A Divine Revelation of Heaven*, Mary Kay Baxter recalls her account of Heaven. During one of her visitations, she states:

> *I remember that the Spirit of God moved continuously in Heaven. It was greater than anything on earth. Things on earth are patterned after things in Heaven, but earthly things can only be shadowy reflections of those in Heaven.*

It is important that as we are actualizing Heaven's existence in us, that we gain the vivid imagination of the continuous movement and transactions going on all around us. Though we cannot see it with our eyes, we are walking in an open Heaven and God's influence is ready to be unleashed through constant demand and acknowledgement being placed on it.

That's one of the first steps to living in an open Heaven, acknowledging that it's there and that continuous movement is going on all around you. In order to live in an "open Heaven" you have to become "open-minded." Unleash yourself to expect, believe, and imagine that Heaven is within and surrounding you, and at anytime God can influence your reality by faith. The more consciously aware you become of the atmosphere of Heaven in you, the more likely you are to began placing demands on the supernatural life you're supposed to be living. Part of what makes your royalty official is the right you have to Heaven's open doors. When God seated you with Christ, it was an open door for you to continually experience a readily available Heaven.

Remember that the Kingdom functions primarily by doors. Those doors come in opportunities that flow from the influence of Heaven's open doors. You have a right to prosper in this earth and bring the divine rule and jurisdiction of Heaven into every arena of your life. Every time you confess something there is an open door. When you pray a door opens and even when you sing doors are opening all around you.

You have the authority to leverage Heaven's open door system to literally produce opportunity no matter where you are in life. You can make streams of water spring forth in a deserted season by placing royal demand on the harvest of Heaven's influence waiting to break forth within you. You are an open door because you are a royal representative of Heaven, and within you is the nature of God the King. You can influence anything to produce the most favorable outcomes at anytime no matter the season you're in.

You have the authority to leverage Heaven's open door system to literally produce opportunity no matter where you are in life.

This means you're not supposed to be waiting on "your time;" you're supposed to be seizing or "redeeming the time" by using

> **You have the authority to leverage Heaven's open door system to literally produce opportunity no matter where you are in life.**

those divine doors to open physical doors through the supernatural influence of God's throne operating within your heart.

One of the reasons we need to understand this is because Heaven is only as powerful as we think it is. Our perception of what is going on around us is the panoply from which life in the Kingdom manifests itself and emerges in our life.

In other words, our ability to experience extreme Kingdom manifestation is contingent upon our awareness of its activity now. Do you perceive it? Are you really aware that constant spiritual transactions are taking place around you? For all of us the doors are open; however, for many people they remain closed; not between Heaven's gates, but between their ears. We have to actualize and accept this principle.

Right now Heaven has designated open doors that you don't know exist. It's time to become forceful about applying your faith to see them materialize.

As it is in Heaven

Every time you ask God what His will is for you there is a silent reply that echoes endlessly through the time from the statement Jesus made in the Lord's prayer: "let your Kingdom come and let your will be done on earth as it is in Heaven." (Or, may heaven manifest in this earth according to its function in your Kingdom.) In other words God is saying to us, "My will is for you to experience Heaven's reality right here on planet earth." In fact it's your job to teach people how to experience Heaven's real existence while they are in this earth realm.

That's why I describe the Kingdom as God's will being manifested in every realm of your life. God's will is so powerful and supreme that if you can grab a hold to it, a Heavenly enforcement will break forth like you've never seen or experienced.

In the Garden of Gethsemane (Matthew 26:36-46) Jesus prayed this prayer: "Not my will be done but your will be done." Jesus wanted His cup to pass, but not because He didn't want to accomplish His assignment. Though this has been taught as such, it isn't totally true about what's happening in this passage. Earlier in Jesus' ministry He prayed Heaven to earth by enforcing God's will through His Kingdom prayer. Therefore, He knows that even in the face of this adversity and difficult time, no matter how it may seem He can strategically draw strength from God's will because He had legally enforced it in the earth.

So, Jesus wanted His cup to pass because of what He was about to drink. Remember the scripture says, "You shall drink poison and not die." Jesus was going to drink from the cup of poison or death.

He was about to "become a curse" (Galatians 3) so the Blessing could flow to you and I. That cup is not His wine, it is death's wine, and it represents the contract Adam made with death.

When Jesus prayed, "Let this cup pass," He was praying out of the strength of His own will. But when He prayed that God's will be done He was drawing from the strength of God's will. We have to learn to draw from God's will, because that is what Heaven enforces.

So when Jesus draws from God's will, it is because He knows God's will is much stronger than His, and in order to drink this cup or partake in this contract, He was going to need a power much greater than His. That power was Heavenly influence being enforced through God's will.

In fact this is so true that after Jesus prayed God's will, the Bible says, "Angels came and ministered to Him" or they "revived Him." What did they revive Him with? The abundance of Heaven's influence through the abounding grace of God's will.

When God sees us He sees Himself. That means we are a mirror reflection of Him. This also means that His will is automatically ours, or more specifically, we have direct access to His will to overcome any obstacle we face. That will enforces Heaven in any circumstances.

You may find yourself wondering if you can do what God has called you to do. You may have a vision so big you're starting to say to yourself "Let this cup pass from me." Don't be intimidated by how big the dream is. Stay focused on the ready availability of Heaven's open doors to you. Stay reminded of God's supreme power and will in you ready for you to draw from it.

If it's taking time to pray an extra hour, draw from God's will. If it's taking more time to listen to faith teaching and Kingdom teaching, draw from God's will. God has put tool after tool in front of us to help us and encourage us to continually draw from Heavenly influence through the divine power of His sovereign will. Remember no one can ever out-influence God's will.

Let His will influence yours. Allow Heaven to invade your territory through the conscious reality of God's will waiting for you to access it. If you do, you'll begin to speak these words to every situation and every circumstance: "As it is Heaven so let be in the earth (my life). And I promise you, according your faith (the law of faith working for you) it will "be done" for you.

The "Open Door" Policy

It's very easy to miss out on opportunities of Heavenly influence. So many doors are open to us if we could just perceive correctly God's direction for us. Thank God for the Holy Spirit who, through constant obedience and seeking, will award us with divine revelation of how to leverage each and every benefit of our royal position in this life.

One of those benefits is being able to rely on Heaven's open door power to shift things in our favor right now. I call it God's "open door policy." Looking back at God's promise to give us gates or doors that remain open, I want to bring another point into the picture: the flow of Heaven's energy and influence in our lives gives us the ability to attract good things.

I want to be clear that God's open door policy states "no matter what, no matter the season (neither day or night), we will always be able to function in His open door power so that men will bring us wealth of the nations (Isaiah 60:11). Or as I like to put it, "so that we will draw and attract to us anything we desire." The "wealth of the nations" isn't just financial prosperity; it is the overflow of favor and opportunities afforded to every Kingdom citizen. That's wealth in the Kingdom.

Now, it is also important that we understand that God doesn't say how these doors will show up. Sometimes we aren't aware of open doors because they don't show up the way we expect them to. God's open door policy is not based on how the opportunity shows up, only that the opportunity is presented.

What does this have to do with our ability to attract good things? Well, sometimes people don't realize that their influence to draw good things is working, because they are looking for large enormous doors to jump right in their face. That doesn't happen all the time.

Even so, Jesus says out of our heart we bring forth good things. We can literally draw and attract great things if we can tap into Heaven's abundant treasures within. So if we can shift and then focus our paradigm to the nature of Heaven's active rule within us, we will be more discerning about doors God is presenting to us. When you declare a thing, it is established (Job 22:28). However, are you really paying close attention to see if what you said is showing up?

Most people miss doors because they aren't "aware" that from the moment they opened their mouth Heaven has been transacting business on their behalf. And because your gates are always open, you need to always be paying attention or looking for opportunity. That's right, you should be seeking out opportunity. I know we have always been taught, "Opportunity knocks at your door." The truth is, opportunity doesn't come knocking on your door until it knows where you live.

Opportunity doesn't come knocking on your door until it knows where you live.

Opportunity doesn't come knocking on your door until it knows where you live.

That's what you're doing by placing royal demands on Heavenly influence, letting opportunity know what your address is so that it can come and find you. I'm also a strong believer that good things don't necessarily come to those who wait, only the things leftover by those who go after them.

Nevertheless, the Kingdom "laws of attraction" are working for you. It's government policy that cannot be undone or restricted. You just have to get a revelation of God's divine open door policy and began placing demands and making royal decrees out of the sovereign place of authority, which is a Kingdom paradigm of Heavenly influence in your heart.

Pay closer attention to these "open doors" and be willing to walk through them no matter how they may show up. Regardless of your season, be reminded that you have the ability to produce the rivers of Eden's Garden, because the Blessing restored to you all the rights of Eden's provision policy.

Confessions for Divine Influence

- I am an open door!
- I am constantly standing in an Open Heaven.
- I place a demand on God's open door policy and command Heavenly influence.
- My gates are always open and I attract good things.
- Heaven is always open for business, therefore opportunity is always going to find me.
- I announce that favor finds me from all places.
- I command open doors that flow from the north, south, east, and west.
- I am Heavenly influence.
- I am divine influence financially, relationally, emotionally, mentally, physically, and spiritually.
- I receive every opportunity and open door God has extended to me through His grace.
- Men are bringing me the wealth of the nations.
- I am wealth attraction.
- According to God's open door policy no doors are ever closed to me.
- I am thriving in divine favor, options and opportunity.
- I declare that I do have a revelation of the day and therefore today is my day!

How Kingdoms Operate

So what is an open heaven? An open heaven is a divine access point for supernatural manifestation. The Kingdom functions by these divine access points which becomes the breeding ground for manifestation of miracles, signs, wonders, and any other kind of supernatural breakthrough. I like to refer to these spiritual doors as "power points." When you access "power points" you are in position to unleash an abundant flow of Heaven's reality into active perpetuation.

A power point can come in the form of an agreement you make with God or a clear instruction you were able to gain through revelation and, by following through on that instruction you were able to produce a harvest. That's how Heaven manifests on earth, through power points of divine law, agreement, obedience, and great acts of faith. When someone hits those power points they give Heaven permission to influence the earth.

Something we must be sure to examine though is that gates not only represent entry points but they can also represent restricted access. What I mean is when Jesus said, "I must work while it is day for no man can work while it's night." Remember the gates were the place of business transaction and marketplace activity? Well, one thing about business gates at that time is when the sun went down, the gates were closed so that no would could "enter" the city or "gain access to the city." That was at nighttime.

So when Jesus said He must work while it is day, that is the revelation of Heaven's rule within you and your present access to it. But when He says you cannot work at night, He is referring to the restricted access a fallen or limited paradigm can have on anyone in the Kingdom.

Although there is no day or night and your gates remain open, they can just as easily be closed or shut if you don't have a "revelation" or paradigm shift concerning your royal position and actual present position in the Kingdom of God. Wake up. Right now you are standing in the throne of grace, favor and mercy. Actualize this and live out of this paradigm of your ascended place.

In other words you need a revelation of the "day." The day is your season as in your *now* season, which is your time of favor or your unlimited authority in Christ. All of that is now! You need to know who you are now and that God's nature has qualified to release Heaven into this earth every day of your life. Don't think with a defeated mentality; that's trying to work at night. You can't access Heaven's gates with that mentality; they will be closed to you.

Stop trying to work to please God or to be righteous; you are righteous through God's supernatural laws manifested in Christ's sacrifice. Again, that's spiritual labor, trying to work at night. Gain a healthy vision and self-picture of yourself. That's your day; that's your abundant life in Jesus. When you choose to operate in this risen paradigm, Heaven is always open to you. Your gates are never closed and you will continually attract good things. You will continually transact Heaven's purposes by divinely influencing every season and opportunity you have.

As we continue looking at these access points to government administration in the earth, we have to remember that access to Heaven's reality is available now and is waiting for you to take your seat and claim your power position in the God class. It's important though, that as we submit our minds to the new Kingdom philosophy and order we understand that the way we think must change.

Every access point to Heaven's open doors or gates has a stone in front of it, like Jacob's well, and removing that stone begins with our philosophy. One of the greatest hindrances to accessing Heaven's open doors is breaking out of traditional, religious belief systems into the unlimited reality of God. In order to do this we must be socialized into the culture and pattern of God by examining bad philosophy that is interfering with Kingdom expansion. Once we do this, we need to delete anti-Kingdom belief systems, no matter how long we've held on to them.

When Jacob was sleeping at Bethel, the Heavens were open to him, just like it is to every Kingdom citizen. However, he was sleeping on a "stone" and that stone is the missing revelation or paradigm that every believer needs in order to actualize and experience the Kingdom reality. By his own confession Jacob said, "I was in the place of the Lord but I was not *aware*." What about you? Are you aware of what you have? Are you really aware of the dynamic opportunity to literally dominate this earth you have through the sovereign purpose of God's will? Right now, like Jacob, the gates are open to you, but you have to receive it, will it, and actualize it.

When you do, no door will ever be closed to you and you will discover the unlimited capacity to rise above limitations in your mind. You will begin drawing from Heaven's open door policy and transacting to you the things you desire in your life.

It's time to win on all levels and in every area of life. The doors are open to you right now. What do you will? The faster you decide, the faster it's going to show up. The Kingdom is within you and you're positioned to reign through your inheritance in Jesus Christ.

You are a king, you are a leader, and you are a dominator. Use every gift you have to master your life and rule your sphere of influence. Remember that every step you take is already predestined to place you in the most favorable outcome. That's empowering grace, your source of winning potential and the life of God flowing in you. Draw from it now and leverage that God-life in you to defy the laws of spiritual gravity in life.

Tap into your blueprint by awakening the sleeping giant and accessing God's roadmap for your success and unlimited prosperity. I believe even now that your atmosphere is changing, your spiritual umbrella is renewing, and you are beginning to attract things to your life that look like God. You are limitless, without boundaries, and capable beyond measure.

You always have the last say and you can always shape your future according to the limitless reality of a Kingdom paradigm. May God's grace be with you and may you experience a life of fullness, wholeness, completeness, and increase. Now is the Kingdom and the power and the glory forever and ever. Amen.